LITERACY CAMPAIGN AND LIBRARIES

(A Handbook for Literacy and Post Literacy Campaign)

Edited By :
Dr. Velaga Venkatappaiah
Three Times National Prize Winner
(For Writing Books for Neo-literates)

Ess Ess Publications

4837/24, Ansari Road, Darya Ganj
New Delhi-110 002
Ph.: 3260807

First Published 1996

ISBN : 81-7000-200-1

Rs. 325/-

Published by
Ess Ess Publications
4837/24, Ansari Road, Darya Ganj
New Delhi-110 002 Ph. 3260807

Composed by
Classic Computer Services
RZ 128/6K Lane No. 9 East Sagar Pur,
New Delhi-110 046 Ph. 5529455

Printed at: Santosh Offset Delhi-35 Ph.: 5117390

NEED OF THE HOUR

Adult Education programme is being organised in India, mostly through voluntary organisations for the last one hundred years or more. Having said and done it has little impact on the increase of growth of literacy in India, may be for the lack of strategy to cover the programme in the country as a whole. However, the Union Government took a policy decision in 1977, and resolved "to wage a clearly conceived, well planned and relentless struggle against illiteracy to enable the masses to play an active role in social and cultural change." The government also thought off, that illiteracy is a serious inpediment to an individual's growth and to country's socio-economic progress. To meet this situation, the Union Government initiated the National Adult Education Programme in 1978 and implemented all over the country. When the programme is going on, the government gave a Mission Approach to Literacy and revamped the programme as National Literacy Mission in 1988, with an objective to impart functional literacy to 80 Million illiterate persons in 15-35 age group-30 million by 1990 and additional 50 million by 1995. This gradually took a shape of Total Literacy Mission and it is now in full swing in the entire country. With all the sincere efforts of the governments at National and State level, and with full support of the voluntary organisations and public it is hoped that the total literacy will be achieved in the country, by the end of this century.

To provide academic and methodological inputs in the programme the government of India established the National Institute of Adult Education (NIAE) in 1991, as an autonomous organisation.

"Through its wide ranging spectrum of activities, NIAE will aim to enchance the knowledge base in adult aducation; improve the quality of research; ensure a strong, two-way relationship between research and practice; improve action, inform policy and engage in theory building; and, develop a sound academic programme.

NIAE will strive to establish adult education as an intar-disciplinary field of study. It will forge links with different disciplines of social sciences. In order to do so, NIAE will play a networking, coordinating and collaborative role with agencies in India and abroad.

NIAE proposes to offer a variety of packages and programmes to suit the diverse needs of people. NAIE has already initiated work in the areas of gender equity in literacy, communication, evaluation issues, social sciences in adult education, population education and post-literacy and continuing education.

NIAE firmly believes in a participatory work style that is informal, unstructured and open to all. It will interact with researchers, policy makers and practitioners through its in-house speaker series, publications, short-term and long-term academic courses, conferences and symposia, library and documentation services, consultancy services and short-term and long-term affiliations at institutional and individual land."

As a part of its programme the National Institute of Adult Education organised a Seminar on the "Role of Libraries in Adult Education" in 1992 in New Delhi. This book is a collection of papers of the said seminar.

As a person, who is associated with the adult education programme for the last three decades, and as a person participated in the Seminar, felt the need for bringing these valuable papers into light and to make use of them by the people of literary programmes.

I must be grateful to my friends Prof. J.A. Wajid, Hon' Consultant and Shri Avik Ghosh, the Semior Fellow of the NIAE for giving me the great opportunity to participate in the Seminar.

I hope that this book will be of great use for the resource persons of Total Literacy campaign at all levels.

V. Venkatappaiah
Editor

CONTENTS

OUR CONTRIBUTORS

Ansari, Prof. S. Dr. Zakeer Hussein Library, Jamia Milia Islamia, New Delhi-110 025

Barua, Dr. B.P. Formerly Director, Raja Rommohun Roy Library Foundation, Calcutta-700 064.

Deepa Das. Project Director, MODE Research Project.

Kalia, D.R. Former President, Indian Library Association, Delhi.

Kaula, P.N. Emiritus Professor, Lucknow University, C 239 Indira Nagar, Lucknow-226 016.

Khanna, Dr. S.N. Director, Delhi Public Library Delhi-110 006.

Khan Suhail. Consultant, Gurgaon, Haryana-112 001.

Krishan Kumar, Dept. of Library and Information Sciences, University of Delhi, Delhi-110 007.

Kumar, Dr. P.S.G. Head, Department of Library and Information Science, Nagpur University, Nagpur-400 010.

Joshi, Prof. N.N.

Laxmi Reddy Dr. M.V. National Institute of Adult Education, New Delhi-110 002.

Mohan Rao, Dr. C.K. National Institute of Adult Education, New Delhi-110 002.

Neela Jagannadhan. Indira Gandhi National Open University, New Delhi-110 068.

Raju, Dr. GVSLN. Dept. of Library and Information Science, Andhra University, Visakhapatnam-530 003.

Sachdeva, J.L. Director, Indian Adult Education Association, New Delhi-110 002.

Singh, Dr. R.S.P. Librarian, State Central Library, Patna.

Srivastava, A.P. Librarian, Delhi Library System, University of Delhi-110 007.

Tilak Mukherjee. Director, MODE Research Project.

Varsha Das. Joint Director, National Book Trust, India, New Delhi-110 016

Venkatappaiah Dr. V. Former Vice President, Indian Library Association, Ithanagaram, TENALI-522 201, A.P.

1

ADULT EDUCATION AND LIBRARIES

Prof. P.N. Kaula

INTRODUCTION

One of the pillars on which the progress of a nation rests is the assumption of the educability of a person, that it is possible deliberately to imporve and sophisticate his/her ability to make rational decisions on private and public affairs. There are powerful forces that challenge the very foundations of democracy and progress. Unless the individual learns to control these forces and use them for peaceful purposes, the future of humanity is in great danger. If we are not able to control the passions which cause mutual hatered, illwill and distrust among the people, the nation may not be able to hold together and may give rise to those elements which may endanger the very constitutional set up of the country. On the other hand if we are, able to control our impulses and direct them into creative and useful channels, we may enter into a new era of peace, understanding, development and of undreamt prosperity.

1 ROLE OF ADULT EDUCATION:

This challenge can be met by awakening in the people a sharp realisation of their responsibility. To achieve this, we fall back on *education* as the only effective instrument for giving faith and courage in educating and re-educating the human race with a view to initiating it into better way of living. Man must learn new skills and techniques and also introduce such changes in the way of living, thinking and working. He or she must cultivate those habits, attitudes and social behavious which will enable him or her to discharge his or her responsibilities as a citizen. Adult education has an important role to play in creating such a sense of unity, oneness and responsibilities among the people.

The interminable arguements over education in the country have not for many decades been over *whether* to educate, but over *how* to educate (including here both method and subject matter) and *how* much education is a citizen's "right" -whether at the higher levels to concentrate self-consciously on the development of an elite group of leaders or to bring culture in all its phases to the masses of men. By and large, Indian, education has been an experiment in mass education at all levels of its structured expression. It aims at the provision of opportunities for mature individuals to continue to learn at all levels. Adult Education is particularly concerned with the provision of such opportunities.

1.1 Continuing Education for Adults

The provision of opportunities for adults to continue learning is desirable because they retain the capacity to benefit from them; it is also socially and economically necessary. Society in all its multifacious aspects is run by adults who of necessity must constantly make decisions on questions at issue of a private or public nature as they arise. The quality of the adults as operators and decision makers. Therefore, decisively influence the nature and quality of our life in the present and the future. Adult education, properly conceived, contributes towards insuring that the quality of the adults, the productiveness of their operations and the value of their decisions are as high as can be achieved by institutional means. Thus there underlies in adult education the same idea that underlies *all* education: that it is a means for improving the *quality* of the individual and society. Continuing education covers the traditional as well as formal education.

1.2 Cognate Concepts

Besides the concept of continuing education, there have been experiments like social education, fundamental education, community education and distance education. Social education improves the individual's ability to group life. It includes remedial, vocational, recreational, health, social skills and self-development education for achieving higher standards of life through society or social groups. It also absorbs the content of adult education and gives it a social orientation. Fundamental education is preparation of children or adults without opportunity for traditional formal schooling for effective participation in community life through instructions in basic facts and skills as of literacy, agriculture, dwelling, hygiene and citizenship. Distance education provides extension of educational opportunities; and general education, liberal education, science education, technical education, vocational education and research programmes are offered through distance education. The courses are more structured at lower levels than at higher levels. In recent years distance education programmes are also extensively used by industries to train their staff. These are efforts to make education of adults more market oriented. Multimedia including electronic media and printed lessons are extensively used in distance education.

1.3 Library Extension Work

Librarians contribute actively to the development of the adult reader's understanding of learning and literature. The provision of libraries immediately following school age cannot he ignored. Only by special work with adolescents will it be possible to throw a bridge across the gap between the activities of the school and the adult's self-education.

Library extension work aims at extension of normal work of the library (the provision of books, book and information service, and reference service, etc.) into other related and associated areas such as the provision of lectures, eshibitions, film display, musical and dramatic activities, etc., so as to reach more and more people. The extension of the normal work of the library includes adult education activities as well.

2 MAIN TASK OF ADULT EDUCATION

The main task of adult education is to help the adults with or without formal education who are desirous to remedy their earlier shortcomings in education. They require individual guidance in their health, vocational and family problems. The most desirable aim is overall self-development.

Long back E.M. Hutchinson, Secretary of the National Institute of Adult Education stated in his paper submitted to the international Conference on Adult Education in Denmark.

"Adult education is taken to mean those forms of education which are undertaken voluntarily by mature people which have as their aim the development, without direct regard to the encouragement of social, moral and intellectual responsibility within the framework of national, local and world citizenship".

2.1 Agencies of Adult Education

Organisations like religious institutions, public organisations, schools, colleges, universities, museums, business organisations, labour organisations, clubs and libraries are suitable for promotion of adult education programmes. For the purpose of this address, the role of libraries in adult education has been specified.

3 LIBRARY AS AN EFFECTIVE FORCE

The library as an effective force in adult education is based on the three assumptions.

1. Adults can learn;
2. It is essential that adults do learn; and
3. The library is in a strategic position to help the adults to learn.

3.1 The stable Agency for Adult Education

The existence of a public library, particularly a free public library, free in the sense that its resources and services are available to its citizens, is in itself an affirmation of the community's belief in the capacity and willingness of the individual citizen to continue purposively to educate himself throughout his life. It is in the words of Dr. S.R. Ranganathan, an agency for life-long education-an agency for universal and perpectual self-education. It is the only stable agency to instruct, inform and mould minds and lives of people. For this purpose it makes accessible the story of human aspirations, achievements recorded in books and allied materials; and it is to books which all intelligent men must turn constantly for information, recreation, instruction and consolidation.

The library provides adult education service under six general categories of service:

1. Supplying of books, films, recordings, tapes and other learning materials;
2. Planning the education activities;
3. Advising the community on subjects, methods and materials;
4. Training the readers and librarians in skills and techniques necessary to adult education activities;
5. Informing the opportunities available through men and materials; and
6. Doing all possible activities to further the adult education.

3.2 Adult Education Activities of Public Libraries

The Library has to play an important role in adult education. The public libraries in the United States carry out adult education activities which are grouped in six broad categories, namely supplying; planning; advising and counselling; training; informing; and performing activities. The activities are given below under each group according to the role played by the library and stated in the publication *Adult Education Activities in Public Libraries* of the American Library Association.

3.25 Informing Activities

Here are the activities in which library gives information to individuals or agencies on reques or on its own.

1. Maintains a central source of information about the adult education opportunities or activities being offered by adult education agencies and informal groups in the community.
2. Maintains an information service about films and other audio-visul resources available to community groups.
3. Maintains a service to provide information about individuals in the community who are willing to speak to or work with community groups as resource people.
4. Promotes and publicizes to the community the library's young adult and adult education services and activities which the library provides alone or in cooperation with other adult education agencies and community groups.

3.26 All work relating to the Activities at the Library

Given hereunder are the activities which the library organizes and presents programmes of all types:

1. Presents book reviews and talk on related books by a library staff member and book talk programme under library sponsorship (not including talks to elementary and secondary school classes).
2. Plans, organizes, administers, and maintains the library's own programmes or activities based on books and other printed materials.
3. Plans, organizes, administers, and maintains the library's own programmes or activities based on film materials.
4. Plans, organizes, administers, and maintains the library's own programmes or activities based on musical or non-musical recordings.
5. Utilizes one or more of the library's adult education services to emphasize a special subject.

6. Plans and develops or utilizes educational programmes on radio stations and TV networks.
7. Plans and presents or utilizes educational programmes on television stations.
8. Emphasizes and concentrates the library's adult or young adult educational services for the benefit of a special interest group(s) in the community.
9. Administers a demonstration project of an adult education activity.
10. Develops and administers a cooperative film or recording services for libraries.
11. Initiates, directs, and/or participates in continuing studies of adult education need and resources in the community.
12. Acts as a producer of materials for adult education projects by request or on its own initiative.

3.27 Additional Activities not Covered

The field of adult education activities is a product of the cultural process of the various groups. Since the communities differ in outlook and character, it is but natural that these activities also differ accordingly. In view of the Indian requirements, the following activities will have to be added to the last group of activities. Many of the activities given in preceeding paras may not be found suitable to our situations.

1. Promotion of literacy;
2. Providing recreational facilities;
3. Organizing study groups, secular or religious;
4. Holding poetical symposia, etc.;
5. Arranging radio and TV programmes;
6. Organising *Kirtans* and *Kathas*;
7. Holding competitions of all types of activities conducted;
8. Teaching good hobbies;
9. Imparting vocational training; and
10. Working with other institutions in various fields to enlist their support for library programmes.

3.28 Libraries and Fundamental Education

All human beings in a modern society should complete a certain minimum of education, i.e., elementary education, in their childhood. If due to some reason or the other some individuals have been deprived of the opportunity of getting elementary education, the deficiency should be remedied later in adult life. Hence the elementary education for adult is generally called remedial education and more aptly named by Unesco-fundamental education.

Libraries play significant role in promotion of fundamental education. It helps in the work of elementary education in two ways. In the first place, it helps a person while he is acquiring reading skills. A library must therefore keep lists of graded reading materials in different subjects of interest to adults. Secondly, once a man becomes literate, the library must see what he does with his newly acquired skills; what kind of reading materials he is interested in; whether he is able to derive benefits from it; whether it conforms to the social cultural and political norms and values set up by him and his community he lives in.

4 GROWTH OF ACTIVITIES

4.1 Development in United States

The concept of adult education activities was earlier promoted by the Society for the Diffusion of Knowledge in UK and specified in Thomas Dick's book on the *Improvement of Society for the Diffusion of Knowledge*, first published in USA in 1933 in Harper's "Family Library". The main analysis of this work was specified as under:

1. Influence of knowledge in dissipating supersititious and vain fears;
2. On the utility of knowledge in preventing diseases and fatal accidents:
3. On the influence which a diffusion of knowledge would have on the progress of science;

4. On the pleasures connected with the pursuit of science;
5. On the practical influence of scientific knowledge and its tendency to promote the comforts of general society;
6. On the influence of knowledge in promoting enlarged conceptions of the character and perfections of the deity.
7. On the beneficial effects of knowledge on moral principles and conduct;
8. On the utility of knowledge in relation to the future world;
9. On the utility of general knowledge in reference to the study of divine revalation;
10. Miscellaneous advantages of Knowledge;
    - Lead to first estimates of human character;
    - Enable people to profit by their attendance in public instruction;
    - Introduce a spirit of tolerance;
    - Vanquish the antipathies of nations;
    - Promote the union of the christian church;
11. On the importance of connecting science with religion.

Americans also used the Mechanics Institute idea, but turned it into a combination of library, lecture and vocational training institution far more than the British model. The establishment of Mercantile Libraries followed by the formation of Mechanics and Apprentices Libraries extended the influence of adult education activities across the Atlantic. The Chautauqua Movement in 1891 staressed that "the principle now so generally accepted that education is the privilege of all, young and old, rich and poor, that mental development is only begun in school and college, and *should be continued through all of life*".

Prof. H.B. Adams stated:

"The thought of higher education for the people through libraries, which are the highest of high schools, is in the air and sooner or later will find lodgment in all our great towns and cities. It is not enough to connect public libraries with the work of the public schools. You must connect your institutions with the educational wants of the people. There should be in every great community organized instruction, through public libraries, for the graduates of public schools, for persons past the school age, for mechanics and working classes in general. Desultory reading and individual use of the public library are not sufficient. There must be methodic and continuous work under proper guidance. There must be concentration of energy on the part of both readers and managers in our public libraries".(1)

4.11 *University Extension Services*

University extension services in 1950 onwards were set out under eleven heads: (2)

1. Correspondence teaching;
2. Lecture services;
3. Summer-school programs;
4. Extension classes;
5. Press and publication services;
6. Evening-school and resident-center activities;
7. Library lending services;
8. Film and visual-aid services;
9. Conference, institute, and short-course activities;
10. Broadcasting services;
11. Special services for communities, institutions, and other interest and professional groups.

4.12 *Symbiotical Relation*

It has been so often emphasised that libraries and adult education have, in theory, what the biologists call a symbiotical relation, which has eleborated the role the libraries play in adult education. Melvil Dewey wrote in 1888:

"Library is a People's University: This often quoted phrase should be made a fact in your library. To every citizen of the state this splendid collection in its splendid home, all paid by the state, should be the real university" where any person may find information on any subject."(3)

This proposal of Dewey was enough to make the library an active participant in adult education. He also tried to apply Herbert Bexter Adm's University-extension idea in the library situation. Following Dewey's pharse of 'People's University' in 1888, Alvin Johnson surveyed the role of public libraries and adult education 1938 and emphasised on........ development of the public library into a permanent centre of adult education informally, a people's university". Carnagie spreading of the idea of 'Readers Advisory Service' to libraries, that had not formally been adopted by libraries. American Library Association sponsored "American Heritage" programme by conducting book-discussion programmes and reading-discussion programmes which helped growth of adult education activities from public libraries. The Association also appointed Audio-visual Board to "take information and ideas to large number of people whom books are not reaching." ALA also recognised the fundamental place with workers education should occupy in the public library programme of adult education.

The all-out adult education activities by public libraries in United States has been appreciated by Glen Burch, then Assistant to the Director of the American Association for Adult Education in the following words:

"I believe that today more and more public librarians... have an understanding of an interest in community problems and are capable of actively sharing in community organization efforts... In some instances entire library systems have chalked up impressive records in community leadership".

4.2 Analogy of other countries

Other developed countries have also recognised the role of libraries in adult education. In UK adult education activities were promoted by National Book League and its branches through the efforts of librarians, for holding lectures about and the discussion of books. Almost all public library authorities have lecture halls and/or meeting rooms which are used for adult education activities and in carrying out adult education programmes. Danish Public Library movement have recognised the effective role of libraries in adult education activities by emphasising as follows:

"Public Libraries should the general education of the people at every stage of development, and support and supplement the work done in schools... Further they should supplement and directly support free work for popular education (lectures and study circles). Public libraries are thus libraries for the whole population".

5 SITUATION IN INDIA

5.1 Pioneering Efforts

Public Library structure in India has been weak and much emphasis has not been given in their role to promote adult education. The library system in Baroda has promoted the role of libraries for adults (1910-1913) followed by Andhra Pradesh where an organised movement for rural library service, field worker activities were promoted through the efforts of Iyyanki Venkata Rammanayya-recognised as the 'Architect of Public Library Movement' in India. He wrote on libraries and Adult Education and discribed the key role of public libraries in promoting literacy and adult education. He also launched on "Library pilgrimages" and emphasised the role of library as People's University.(5)

5.2 Experiments in Education

Education in India has been in a melting pot. Several experiments have been made to reform the structure of education. In 1947-48 we had limited number of institutions of formal educaton which have increased quantitatively but the plan outlay on education decreased steeply to 0.5 percent in the Sixth Plan. However, the unprecedented and unplanned growth of institutions at various levels of education has resulted in enormous increase in expenditure and decline in the quality of education. Literacy and adult education programmes have been renewed involving more people into it. It is yet to be seen if it would be a success. The policy document *"Challenges of Education"* admitted:

"Education system has failed to bring about social transformation... change in education system has been of a degree and not of a kind".

5.3 Adult Education Activities

Adult Education is a permanent necessity for citizenship. An uneducated democracy is not only a failure but a positive danger to the state. Hence, our educational efforts must be primarily concentrated on the improvement of the intellectual capacity of adults in the country. Public library is the coordinating centre of adult education activities to eradicate illiteracy and promote adults education.

The Unesco Public Library Manifesto stating "the profound faith in the value of book service to the common people of a nation through public libraries", runs as follows:

"The public library is a product of modern democracy and a practical democracy's faith in universal education as life-long process. Though primarily intended to the educational needs of adults, the public library should also supplement the work of schools in developing the reading tastes of children and young people, helping them to become adults who can use books with appreciable profit".

Public libraries should be established and maintained under the clear authority of law supported wholly and mainly from public funds and should be open for free use on equal terms to all members of the community regardless of occupation, creed, caste or race. The establishment, maintenance and development of public libraries should be of a definite pattern based on legislation.

5.4 Efforts of Dr. Ranganathan

Dr. S.R. Ranganathan "Father of Library Science in India" has worked incessantly for the development of public library structure in India. He published the following works depicting his vision and plans for public library development of India:

1. National Library system: A Plan for India, 1947
2. Postwar Reconstruction of Libraries for India, 1947
3. Rural Adult Education, 1949
4. Library Development Plan-A Thirty Year Plan for India, 1950
5. Education for Leisure, 1946, 1948, 1954
6. Social Education Literature, 1932
7. Library Service for All, 1966
8. National Grid of Libraries based on Legislation, 1972
9. Public Library System 1972
10. Indian Library Manifesto, 1991

5.5 Apathy of the Government

All works of Dr. Ranganathan given above and others laid emphasis on nation-wide grid of libraries. He advocated the setting up of the National Central Library which has not been established till today. The Five Year Plans speak of the apathy of the Government towards library development. The establishment of National Central Library provided in first two Five Year Plans and modified in the Third Plan has yet to see the light of the day. An integrated national library system with many cultural, political, economical and educational snag of keeping libraries separate from education in the state subiect list should have been rectified long back.

The government did not draw up a national policy on education soon after our independence. It woke up only in 1968 and formulated a policy which was not implemented. In produced a document "*Challenge of Education-A policy perspective*". But the document prepared by experienced and top educationists in the country had ignored the role of libraries in education, protests by professional organisations and individual librarians were launched. This resulted in the appointment of the National Committee to draft the National policy on Library and Information System. The Committee with which this speaker was associated, delivered the final draft into the hands of the

Union Minister for Human Resource Development on 30 May 1986. But no implementation has taken place till this date. The revised draft of the National Policy on Education contained a paragraph on the general improvement of libraries and book culture. This paragraph was interpolated on the basis of representation. Why did this happen, is anybody's guess! Eight states have enacted library laws for public library development of which three states have yet to implement the provisions of the library Acts adopted.

5.6 Programme on Adult Education

The Government of India also launched a National Programme on Adult Education in 1978 without specifying the role of public libraries in this programme. This speaker wrote to the then Union Minister of Education to spell out the role of libraries in adult education. The reply came that the matter has been referred to the concerned division and that information would be given. But no information was received from the concerned division in the Ministry. In 1983, it was revealed by the Director of Education of Planning Commission that Rs. 45 crores had been sunk on this myth of Adult Education. That is how the programme worked. One of the reasons of the failure had been that no role of public libraries in the programme had been specified this snag in this programme.

6 DELHI PUBLIC LIBRARY ACTIVITIES

Delhi Public Library was set up by Unesco in 1951 as a Public Library Pilot Project. It was specified in the agreement between Unesco and the Government of India that the library was to carry out the policy of the UNESCO Public Library Manifesto. Consequently it became a cultural community centre. It organised interested readers groups like literature study group; social study group; Health Hygiene Group; and Homoeopathic Study Group. The Library has encouraged recreational activities and has set up rural libraries, Gramophone Record Library and Deposit Stations for service to prisoners, indoor patients of hospitals, service to sport lovers besides an effective Mobile Library Service to supply books at the door steps of readers. It has also set up a Braille Library for the blind people. It was the first library to provide free library service to readers and has got the credit of being the busiest public library in Asia.

7 SOME OTHER ISSUES

7.1 Role in Distance Education

India has started open University education system from Andhra Pradesh when it established the Open University. With the establishment of Indira Gandhi National Open University in New Delhi with centres in many parts of the country, the role of its library in adult education activities has come up for consideration. Since the distance education is to meet the growing social and individual educational needs and also the need to create a learning society, it should be capable of providing opportunities for life long education and training for the work force. The important role in extending educational opportunities to larger sections of adult population has been recognised. There are models on distance education before us. The basic model is the Open University work of Britain which promoted India to have similar experiment. Another model is that of Australia. The Australian model is based on covergence of the conventional and the distance system of education. It has shown that the distance mode of education can be used for education of the learners of any age group. There is increasing use of electronic media in distance education in Australia, though they have understood its limitations. printed medium is to be the primary media followed by audio cassettes. Computers are also used for providing two-way communication in Australian model which India shall have to use in due course. Coordination and rationalisation of distance education among provides in India would be necessary without sacrificing the advantages of plurality, competition and experimentation. The libraries in distance education shall have to orient their activities to achieve the goal of distance education.

7.2 Training for Adult Education Activities

There are two special groups in the adult population that merit the special attention of curriculum planners-young adults and the again adults. Each group requires education geared to its unique problems and aspirations. The dominant aspiration of the young adult is to gain status in the world of adults. Discussion groups in community problem, leadership training and human relations are needed by them. Action programmes related to civic affairs are necessary. Classes in vocational training, home making and parent education help him prepare for his financial and family future. The aging group either in retirement or facing it need training in personal adjustment to leisure, participation in arts and crafts, study of health and budgeting problems.

The library can assist in the following tasks:

1. Planning the programme to be offered;
2. Recommending priorities to shape the programme;
3. Developing good public relations;
4. Surveying the educational needs;
5. Keeping the adults well informed with wide and upto date material.

The problem of training of personnel for adult education activities in the libraries is a challenging one. The question is what should be the content of the training and when and where it should be given. Library should be a joint not given this subject due place. There should be a joint collaboration of Indian Adult Education Association with the Indian Professional associations to work out a detailed programme of instruction.

In library science courses some more attention has to be paid in library Extension Activities to include the work of adult education and the training required for that purpose.

7.3 Lack of Reading Habit

The habit of reading among the adults is not much. It has to be increased so that adults are prepared to have self-study. The lack of reading habit is due to the following:

1. The inability of the neoliterates to read, comprehend, follow instruction and lack of self confidence and hesitation to take up the book and read;
2. Lack of books in the writing of which actual skills and abilities achieved by the neoliterates as a whole has been kept in mind;
3. Lack of time on the part of the people;
4. Lack of well-maintained libraries;
5. Lack of favourable borrowing facilities;
6. Lack of trained library personnel to serve the adults.
8. The Road Ahead

Public Libraries must concentrate more largely now than they have in the past on materials and services for persons who have some purpose in their reading. Libraries must be increasingly aware of social economic, political and cultural objectives and must learn how to use their materials and personnel to help people advance towards those objectives. These objectives are good race relations, religious tolerance, international cooperation, and good citizenship. The library should change its role from mere book-delivery library to the learning material centre.

We cannot fight ignorance and supersitions or increase our efficiency or broaden our interest or guard the citadal of democracy or build the edifice of the good life unless we become an education nation in the deeper sense of the word and for that purpose, reading with discrimination and intelligence is a basic condition. The foundation of it must be laid through the Adult Education movement with the assistance of the public libraries.

The creation of interest in reading and the sound reading habit depend not on teaching or a library but the availability of good books suited to different age groups and the manner in which the library service is organised. It calls for cooperation between writers, publishers, educationists, and librarians. That should be the further road ahead.

REFERENCES

1. DITZION: Arsenals of Democratic culture, p. 186.
2. CREESE James: Extension of University Teaching, p. 194.
3. RIDER FREMONT: Melvil Dewey, p. 88.
4. CRATTAN C H: In Quest of Knowledge, p. 168.
5. JOHNSON Alvin: The Public Library-A People's University, p. 61.
6. RAMANAYYA I.V: Light of the Library p. 41-47.

2

CONCEPTUALISATION OF ADULT EDUCATION AND LIBRARIES

Prof. Anand P. Srivastava

WHAT AND WHY OF ADULT EDUCATION

The definition and scope of adult education appear not to be very simple and exact. A better comprehension of the difition and scope of adult education could be obtained for which we have to understand the features of modern society by differentiating it from the earlier eras is the progress of man in his evolution. It is said that the biological evaluation of man has taken about two million years and it is also calculated that the cultural evolution of man is of about twenty thousand years. During the cultural evolution the man has lived in cave culture, in agricultural society, in industrial society and now the mankind is very much in the post industrial information society. There was a time when cave was the centre of life. This era was succeeded by agricultural farm as centre of society. Then, came a period when factory became the centre of a society. It is clearly desernible today that the centre of the modern society is the school, media centre and the library. The process of learning has became essential from cradle to grave. A society that consumes most of knowledge and information is clearly an advanced and powerful society, and a society that consumes least knowledge and information is a backward and weak society. Today, there is a contrast between different societies on the earth. There is clear cut different between the society possessed with knowledge, one had the society dominated by ignorance. Very recently, one had seen the confrontation between the two in the event of the Gulf war, where a group possessing scientific and technological knowledge fought against another group dominated by ignorance and out moded traditional attitudes.

The adult education as a concept originated with the fundamental need that a person worthy of living a modern life should be properly trained in learning processes from the day a child open his eyes upto the day when as an old person his eyes get closed through natural death. The movement of adult education has obtained importance even in those countries where literacy ranges between 90 to 100 per cent. Therefore, literacy is not the exclusive jurisdiction of atult education. Literacy is just the essential means for equiping a person to continue to learn all his life. The sphisticated components of adult education are continuing learning, compensatory learning and learning for development. Adult Education is a movement which enables a modern citizen to live properly in the present day society, just as skills for land ploughing were essential in agricultural society, and training in sword fighting was essential in the feudal society. The concept of adult education in India has to include literacy, but not literacy alone. In India, people with about 16 to 18 years of formal education relapse to the practical stage of illiteracy even after obtaining a university degree.

Therefore, one year's effort in making literate alone cannot make us achieve the goals of adult and continuing education. Through learning materials and other programmes for learning our literacy efforts should make a citizen a learner for life. This kind of learning is, therefore, to be supported through relevant materials and programmes. The relevant materials and programmes should be the component of media centres particularly the libraries. To start with libraries shall have to be attached with schools, community centres and public library unit.

SOME ESSENTIALS FOR ADULT EDUCATION

During the last five hundred years, in developed countries, the new knowledge which got generated was adapted and disseminated for the bebefit of various sections of society at large. This was largely done through "Guttenburg" Device. In the orient this kind of activity started very late, that too, for a microscopic minority, which in turn did not spread and share it with the masses. The result was that the masses remained ignorant of the new knowledge and continued to live with superstition and outdated tradition. The past was not replaced by the present in such societies. Now, it is our endeavour that through various movements, including adult education, the knowledge generated by scientists and scholars is adapted and disseminated to users. Land Grant University and Green Revolution are such examples, which tried to make knowledge functional and useful with the medium of communicators, viz., extension agencies, adult education, libraries, etc. In this process user needs were identified and relevant knowledge was packaged and delivered, which may have been a research report, an information search package, a brochure, a book for literate or neo-literate, a radio programme, a family planning compaign or any other such activity. For effective utilization of knowledge it is necessary that it is properly monitered, screened, indexed, catalogued, packaged and stored in various forms for dissemination. Effective communication is the heart of the process. Libraries and librarians have major roles to play in such a movement.

Our country cannot disseminate unless literature is available for delivery. A study of the western culture shows that school teachers have authored a gread deal of literature for children, neo-literates and the general public; and university and research manpower have authored specialised literature for continuing eudcation of the specialised category of people. Our force of millions of teachers has not been motivated to produce literature for children, neoliterates and the general public. Our learned societies have performed largely inaugural and valedictory functions, and in between election of new office bearers. We have learned associations practically on each discipline but comapred to, say, an European counterpart, we have produced very poorly. Unless, the teaching force, having advantage of vacation is made to produce literature for neo-literates, children and the masses; our adult education movement shall remain at disadvantage. Necessary plans have to be floated for making our teachers to write books, etc. Unless the learned societies and associations compile new knowledge as periodical-progress-manuals, the specialist sector shall remain behind time in acquainting itself with new knowledge. The adult education movement has to collaborate with such agencies for its own success.

Unfortunately, in our country, the price of paper is relatively very high. This factor alone is capable of preventing the progress of adult education movement and life-long learning processes. We must at least example paper from excise duty, so that books, etc., at cheaper rates are made available.

Some agency in our country should acquire from the westers world copies of children's books, books for neoliterates and books for the masses, and let our teachers and specialists study them for adaptation, translation and Indianization, etc. Once suitable manuscripts are produced through quality and inexpensive desk-top printing, the marketing and selling to libraries and schools, etc., at modest cost, should not be difficult. Through a suitable price-control-device private enterprise should also be allowed to produce and market them.

Unless the kitchen of each family becomes a laboratory and the drawing-room becomes a museum and library, the success of adult education, as continuing learning process in life, is not likely to succeed. Educational growth is basically evolutionary in nature. As there had been biological evolution through generations similarly there is educational evolution through generations in a society. It is only the continuing education which can provide proper synthesis between an individual's interests and roles with that of the roles and interests of the society as a whole. Viewing in the global context, our country needs revision and enlargement of older systems of thought, values and knowledge. Empiricist and rationalist have to be blended properly. If monkeys can before eating separate sand from grains, the mankind can certainly learn a lot through adult education. But transmission and transformation of tradition must be attempted for cultural and educational evolution. Here, libraries and media centres shall be the institutions of primary importance.

Unfortunately, whenever, architects and planners even like D.D.A., develop colonies they never provide a place for libraries and media centres in newer posh colonies. A colony, today, in absence of a library/media centre should be equated with a jungle. Adult education authorities should contact the national associations of planners, architects, colonisers, ministry of urban/rural development, etc., for inveriably providing for libraries and media centres. Appeals be made to 'dharamshalas', waqf boards and other religious bodies to provide for libraries and secular media centres even in their existing building. If temples, mosques and churches develop secular libraries and media centres the needed enlightenment movement shall take place in India. Exchange and utilisation of knowledge shall take place in our country, and cut moded institutions shall become modern centres of great importance and value.

Wherever we have school buildings in rural India, even in urban India, place for library and media centre be developed there. By and large we should provide the services of trained librarians, monitoring *pre to post* literacy programmes in villages. Books can reach the villages even on bullock carts, cycles, 'charpaies' etc.

The institution of honorary librarians with nominal honorarium shall have to be disbanded because it shall give no results except formal expenditure of funds, and possibly political benefit to supporters of elected representatives in various political constituencies.

Briefly, a national movement to "learn" has to be launched by the developed sector of our society, with institutional development of universities, schools, hospitals, police stations, tehsil offices and pargana units, blocks etc..

CONTINUATION OF EDUCATION FOR ALL

Through out all earlier times in the human history, until yesterday, the ruling social powers assumed human masses to be universally ignorant and accredited them with having only muscle and dexterity value. It also appears that during ancient times there was deliberately planned policy, adopted by the political and religious powers, which conditioned the human reflex to miss-see and misconceive even the macro-micro cosmic system. It certainly was an emperor and priest conciveace that the mankind was left to think largely about the life after death. But the modern concept of a welfare society wants the mankind to see properly and conceive accurately the present. For these objectives it is essential that continuing education should be for all and the concept of becoming perfect in an instance, by device of touch, should become rare in the present day modern society. The God should not be the only force to make a person behave rightly. The concept "public good" should obtain greater preferance. Therefore, the continuing education on worldly needs and affairs should be for all:

a) For women who is most effective agent for developing the future generation,
b) For man the scientist and scholar,
c) For man the administrator,
d) For man the politician and social leader,
e) For man the farmer and the labourer, who are required to produce.

It must be briefly stated that the knowledge requirement of a farmer and a labourer, for leading fruitful and productive life, is such greater than that of a clerk who gets involved into limited routine activity. The concept of adult and continuing education has emerged to take care of all these categories of learners realising that the quantum and quality of knowledge and information needed during life span cannot be dispeased only in one stroke when the person is attending a school or a college. Acquisition and utilisation of knowledge have to be a lifelong process. It has been estimated that one third population in developed countries is engaged in the task of knowledge and information generation, exchange and utilisation. The sceneario in the third world countries is very poor in this respect. It is in the third world countries that majority of the people are illiterate and ignorant. It is in the third world countries that the population pressure is enormous. It is in the third world countries again that there is tremendous gap between the demand and supply of goods. Therefore, it is in the third world countires that the need for adult and continuing education is immense, and for the very survival of these countries it is essential tht people are equiped to learn and acquire knowledge throughout their living span. Unless this movement is successfully operated there should be no hope for the third would countries to survive. With the availability of computing devices, reprography and printing technologies, satellite techniques and political will, it should not be possible for third world countries to go for the success of adult education movement. About 30 years ago it was my privilege to be the Director of Adult Education in a university which was the pioneer in introducing a Department of Adult Education. Through the vision of its Vice-Chancellor, Dr. Mohan Sinha Mehta, series of lecture programmes were organised which experienced that the masses in large number participated in these programmes. It is certain that if suitable lecture programmes are organised in our village and towns, even the illiterate population shall participate in listening to such lectures of informative value. What the masses are presently listening to are either political lectures or religious sermons. Secular and social knowledge is not reaching to the masses even throught the words of mouth. If we examine the factors that made one category of countries such superior in knowledge consumption than the category of countries where knowledge is least consumed, we shall find the secret of success of the first category in the following phenomena:

a) Origin and growth of children's literature,
b) Utilisation of pre-school years;
c) Creation of adolsence literature and literature for new literates,
d) Shift from teaching to learning treads in schools and colleges,
e) The large scale continuing education programmes,
f) Other academic activities through public libraries, museums, clubs etc.

It must be repeated that unless the kitchen of an educated family becomes a laboratory and the drawing room becomes a museum and a library, the roots of a learning society cannot be planted in a country. The scholarly history, for example of Europe, clearly shows that the perid of of enlightenment, preceded by certain movements and succeeded by ceertain other movements, cultivated strong will for learning in that society. Though higher education came to India around 1800 A.D. and people spent about 18 years in continuation in schools and colleges, they left the portals of the universities only with a piece of paper called a degree, and were deprived of strong learning skills, as were unable to use them in their post-teen years. Very high percentage of people, when asked as to when they read a book last, are invariably heard answering, "It was when he/she took his or her last examination". Such an attitude, and fact of life, make investments in education totally unproductive. Learning shall not thrive in such a society. Hence, due care is to be taken by our adult education movement that merely a year's effort is literacy mission does not result into neo-learning by neo-literates.

ADULT EDUCATION—SOCIAL CULTURAL AND POLITICAL ASPECTS

Through the movement of adult education an attempt is made to equip the people with ability to acquire knowledge and information needed for their living. Since the people are concerned, any conceptualisation must adopt society-centred approach. It is very clear that mental structures of people are formed by different social and cultural settings. The movements of adult education tries for social change and development. Regers has identified 9 middle range prepositions concerning knowledge defusion activities.

They are:

1. Social structure acts to impede or to facilitate the rate of diffusion and adoption of new ideas through system effects.
2. Diffusion can change the social structure of a social system.
3. Power elites act as gatekeepers to prevent restructuring of innovations from entering a sociaol system while favouring functioning innovation that do not immediately threaten to change the system structure.
4. A system's social structure helps determine the nature and distribution of an innovation's consequences.
5. Top-down change in a system, which is initiated by the power elites, is more likely to succeed than is bottom-up change.
6. Bottom-up change involves a greater degree of conflict than top-down change.
7. Bottom-up change is more likely to be successful at times of perceived crisis in a sytem.
8. Bottom-up change is more likely to be useful when a social movement is headed by a charismatic leader.
9. The role of the charismatic leader in a social movement decreases as the movement becomes institutionalized into a more highly structured organization.

An adult education movement must give due consideration to the above factors while trying to equip the masses for acquiring and using knowledge through adult education programmes.

The role of culture in a society is highly important in relation to acquiring and using knowledge. In fact, the culture-attributes largely shape the use of knowledge in a society. It is rightly said that knowledge, as a product of cultural traits, demands that indigenous knowledge system should obtain high priority for dissemination in society. Dissanayake recommends the following points for accommodation efforts based on indigenous knowledge system:

1. Ideas borrowed from the people, and then developed and refined in the light of modern knowledge, have a far greater change of being readily accepted than those imported from outside.
2. The use of culturally sanctioned indigenous knowledge systems promotes bottom-up development.
3. For the development effort to succeed, focus on materials alone is not adequate. Attention needs best be achieved through the harnessing of indigenous knowledge systems.
4. The use of indigenous knowledge systems promotes local skills and initiative.
5. The harnessing of knowledge and skills found among a people tends to increase popular participation in development efforts.
6. Greater attention to indigenous knowledge systems facilitates the adaptation of new technology to suit local needs and conditions.

These points are associated with economic as well as psychological factors that prevail in a society and an adult education worker has to give due importance to these factors.

There is a political dimension of taking knowledge and information to people. Wealth and power relationships have great impact in political life. Even agricultural technology is not nuetral to political implications. The spatial distribution of benefits, even of Green Revolution, have political tones. The Green Revolution is largely the use of biological and chemical knowledge and with their socio-economic impact, it has shaped the political details ina society which may even aggravate social conflicts. "Mandalisation" has recently shows the impact of carrying knowledge to the masses with political details and resulted into aggravation of social conflicts. Since knowledge does provide increase in the output and income redistribution, it results into the restructuring of society with political tones wherein social tension cannot be eliminated altogether.

While we carry knowledge to the people, and equip them to use knowledge in their life, it is not at all without reactions-good or bad-even then, the knowledge has to be carried to the masses and people have to be equiped through adult education movement to acquire knowledge and information for their benefit.

LIBRARY AND MEDIA SUPPORT FOR ADULT EDUCATION

It shall be difficult to establish new libraries exclusively for adult education movement. Why sow seeds if irrigation could not be done? Libraries as institutions are already falling out of monopolistic ownership of parent institutions. national and regional networks are the proof of this trend. Five hundred years ago each home had to manage its own water needs and night lighting equipment. Now we have Water Supply Undertaking and Electricity Supply Corporations, functioning in each viable geographical unit. Why not think of Information and Knowledge Supply Boards in each geographical area for all types of knowledge and information users? We must go for library legislation in remaining states of India. Have a Public library network in districts and cities. Club then with academic libraries particularly school and college libraries. Let there be mobile libraries to reach the commuity at scattered places. After all the Delhi Public Library as a pilot project of Unesco was required to get multiplied in our country. We have to expand our libraries into media centres, with infra-structure to make them real media centres.

We have to develop a phased programme for establishing and/or developing such Library-cum-Media centres in our vast country. A specialist group should be assigned the task to develop suitable blueprint for it in collaboration with various agencies in the field.

REFERENCES

1. Rogers, E.M. Strategies for Planned Change. ed. G. Zaltman and R. Duncan, New York, Wiley. 1977.
2. Dissanayake, W. Understanding the role of the Environment in Knowledge and use... In. ed. George M. Beal, etc. Knowledge Generation, Exchange and Utilisation. New York, Westview, 1987.
3. Srivastava, Anand P. Bio-Tech. and Information Society in India *ILA Buletin No.3, 1990.*

3

LIBRARIES AND ADULT EDUCATION AN HISTORICAL PERSPECTIVE

J.L. Sachdeva

The establishment of libraries in India dates back to 1835 when the first library was set up in Calcutta from private resources. By 1850 the Public Libraries had come into existence in the cities of Bombay, Calcutta and Madras. The first attempt by the Government to provide public library service was made in 1902 when it purchased the Calcutta Public Library and threw it open for the use of general public.

It the matter of rural libraries, the lead was taken by Baroda in early part of the 20th century. Dr. M.Visveswarayya, the architect of modern Mysore (now Karnataka), and Dewan of Baroda had played a significant role in this regard. He believed in education of the masses and initiated a scheme of mass literacy supported by a net work of circulation libraries in rural areas.

With the establishment of provincial Governments in 1937, the literacy and library movement got a boost. The political leaders took an active part in the movement. Bihar spearheaded the movement. The Minister of Education of Bihar, Dr. Syed Mahmud appealed to youth of the Province to "wage an unremitting war against poverty and ignorance". To check relapse into illiteracy a detailed programme of post literacy mainly through cirulating libraries and fortnightly newsheet called "Roshni" (light) was initiated. Several existing libraries were strengthened to start the circulating section. A massive plan of establishing 2500 libraries in Bihar was also worked out by the Mass Literacy Committee. In 1940 nearly 4000 libraries were set up in selected Thanes which started functioning in January 1940 under the supervision of local sub-inspectors of schools. The enthusiasm for literacy Ministries. During the period 1940-44 nearly 8000 libraries were established which was the largest network of libraries in British India.

The pioneering work in the field of public libraries was initiated in thirties with the efforts of Dr. S.R. Ranganathan. With his suggestion some State Governments established Public libraries through legislation. The Central Library and District Libraries were established.

The integral connection between public libraries and adult education was recognised as early as 1949, when delegates from 28 countries met at Elsinore (Denmark) at the International Conference on Adult Education and passed the following resolution "This conference records its recognition of the essential contributions of Museums and Public Libraries to Adult Education. Appropriate to the circumstances of each Member-State, the Conference supports UNESCO's PROCLAMATION that the public library is a living force for popular education, culture and information and recommends its consideration and, as far as possible its adoption in Member States as a basis of policy".

The first systematic attempt to start a public library to meet the needs of neo-literates and less educated people was made in New Delhi with the establishment of Delhi Public Library (DPL) in 1951 with financial and technical support of UNESCO. The library has met the needs of the Metropolis to a great extent. It consists now of a central library, a zonal library, 29 branch/sub branches and community libraries, a braille library, 14 braille mobile service points and seven braille deposit stations, 31 resettlement colony libraries and reading rooms, two hospital libraries, a library in central jail and a network of mobile service stations serving 81 areas and 21 deposit stations in Delhi.

When DPL was established in 1951 it was hoped that such models will be replicated in other parts of the country so that the reading needs of the neo-literates, less educated and the educated could be met. But not much progress on these lines has been made in other parts of the country.

With the advent of the Community Development Projects, a provision was made in the schematic budget of each development block for social education under which old libraries could be supported or new libraries could be set up. A number of libraries were set up under this provision and they served a useful purpose. In most of the States the Social Education Workers looked after the circulating of books and were expected to manage small circulating libraries and the village level workers were to distribute books. However, with the diffusion of social education programmes and abolition of posts of Social Education Workers in many States, the programme of establishing libraries and providing library services received a major setback.

The brightest spot in the library movement after independence has been the establishment of large number of libraries in Kerala. The library movement was started by a voluntary organisation called 'Kerala Granthasala Sangham' which established over 4000 libraries all over the State particularly in rural areas. Kerala on an average has one library for a population of 3000. 50 percent of the libraries have their own buildings which were built up with the initiative of local people. The KGS also started functional literacy project in 1971. The libraries provided accommodation for the classes and other facilities. In 1977 the State Government took control of the KGS and its direct involvement in literacy ended. But it continues to serve the masses thru the book collection and other audio-aids.

The Karnataka State Adult Education Council, Mysore has also done a appreciable work in establishing libraries in different parts of the State. It had established over 3000 rural libraries, 44 Circle libraries and 12 Central libraries. The rural libraries are linked with adult education centres to prevent relapse into illiteracy.

The experiments of Literacy House, Lucknow in the field of rural library service deserve mention. They were Bell Bicycle, Tin Trunk and workers mobile library services. the system of mobile library conceptually is very sound because it provides the right book to the right reader at the doorstep. But the low level of honorarium given to the librarians which does not commensurate with the work involved has not attracted competent and committed people for this work. The librarian is also expected to create urge or habit for reading which in many cases has not been done under the mobile library projects.

The establishment of Jan Shikshan Nilayams (JSNs) under the National Literacy Mission is a significant achievement. The long felt need of institutionalising post-literacy and continuing education has been met. The Nilayam's includes a library, reading room, a communication centre, a recreation centre, etc. The JSN is based on a concept which is highly innovative and if properly organised can surely build the foundation of a learning society.

But it is doubtful whether a part time Prerak who is the main functionary of the JSN will be able to organise the multifarious activities of the Nilayam. The honorarium is too low, there is no provision of money for hiring space. Based on our experience of community centres in rural areas under Community Development Programme, it is high time to have close look at the provision for a JSN. The JSN, if properly funded and organised could go a long way not only in providing reading material for the neo-literates and the less educated but also would be helpful in creating facourable climate for literacy.

The library is the best medium for self education and can serve the need of both neo-literates and the educated. The treasure of knowledge preserved in books can made the life of the people richer and happier, if the same is made available to them in suitable form at convenient place and time.

With the limited resources available in the country it is desirable that existing educational institutions particularly primary schools in the villages shoudl be utilized for adult education and providing library service. There are 5,78,862 inhabited villages in the country. Out of these 3,95,654 villages have a primary school in the village. They should be utilised for imporving the community life and should cencern with the people, their needs, education and recreation. They can effectively provide library and reading room for the community.

The libraries and adult education are complementary and supplementary to each other and both have to be promoted to give the benefits of education to the masses. This role had been very well recognised by the Mohan Sinha Committee on Literacy Among Industrial Workers (1964) which said "The cheapest and most effective and even otherwise the most desirable method of providing the neo-literates adults to keep their literacy skills in working condition is the public library system. The whole scheme of literacy hinges on well-organised library."

An effective public library system could go a long way in meeting the growing educational needs of adults.

REFERENCES

1. Gardner, Frank M. *The Delhi Public Library: An evaluation report.* Paris, Unesco, 1957, 94 p.
2. Houle, Cyril O. *Libraries in Adult and Fundamental Education: The report of the Malane Seminar.* Paris, Unesco, 1951
3. Indian Adult Education Association, *Libraries in Social Education: Report of the Sixth National Seminar, Delhi, September 26-October5, 1955.* New Delhi, IAEA, 1956. 46p.
4. India, Government of India, Committee on Plan Projects. *Report on Literacy among industrial workers.* New Delhi, 1966. 94p.
5. Nagappa, T.R. *Rural Library movement in India.* Indian Journal of Adult Education. Vol.40, No. 9, 1978, pp 17-21.
6. Pallai, K.S. *Adult Education in Kerala: Some innovative Exsperiments:* Indian Journal of Adult Education, Vol.45, No.1-2 1984 pp 7-12.
7. Saxena, J.C.; Sachdeva, J.L. *Eds. National Literacy Mission: Problems and Prospects.* New Delhi, Indian Adult Education Association, 1989, 62 p.
8. Shah, S.Y. *Adult Education in Bihar*, New Delhi, Indian Adult Education Association, 1989, 118p.
9. Venkatappaiah, V. *The NAEP and Public Library.* Indian Journal of Adult Education, Vol. 40, No.4, 1979. pp 43-44.

4

ELECTRONIC MEDIA AND ADULT EDUCATION LIBRARIES

Suhail Khan

It started with radio and television has given a new dimensions to this ongoing social and cultural revolution brought about in India by the electronic media.

The penetration of electronic media into the lives of the masses of our country is as deep as the impact it has over them.

Radio and television have been effectively used for dispersing information, entertaining masses, selling consumer products and even to further political goals.

Electronic media has also been employed for enhancing and supplementing regular courses in formal educational system and has proven its effectiveness.

But when it comes to adult education, this perfect tool has only been tried in a very few and isolated pockets.

With the staggering number of illiterates in India, we must explore all the possibilities. This medium can provide to spread literacy or to widen the horizons of neo-literates.

I was fortunate enough to get an opportunity to conduct and experiment called '*Chauraha*', which was exclusively designed to impart literacy through video based lessons. A workbook was also designed to go along with the video. This combination of video and book has yielded extremely positive results, during its initial testing.

'Chauraha' was successful with its target audiences because of its simple computer aided visuals coupled with appealing nanatives. Learning to write was also made easy by an animated pencil which befriended with the learners and was thus instrumental in removing the initial hesitation shown by almost every adult learner when they try writing for the first time. Television, in this case, proved to be a very effective learning aid.

Exceptional staying power of these video based lessons was also observed in places where the pilot episode and the scripts of 'Chauraha' were pretested.

India has never been a society of book readers. Per capita consumption of paper in our country is still one of the lowest in the world. Instead, we have cultivated a very rich tradition of story-telling which reflects in our folk songs and in our folk music.

This temprament matches perfectly with the possibilities, I want to explore for using the electronic media in adult education.

Adult education libraries is a relatively new concept. The importance and need for such libraries will be increasing very rapidly with the success of the many fast paced literacy campaigns, going on all over the country.

Although a lot of agencies and individuals are busy producing material for the neo-literate, but most of the work is generated in convential point media.

We must exploit the power of electronic media and would that to meet the new challenges in new surroundings of Adult Education Libraries.

Introduction of electronic media into the adult education libraries will have a set of problems of its own such as:

- Biggest of them all-additional costs
- Training people in the libraries to operate and maintain the associated hardware.
- Access to a place suitable for operating and safe keeping the hardware and software.
- Availability of electricity etc. etc.

At this point cost of hardware and the expenditure involved in generating the software seems to be a big burdle.

Besides this, a psychological barrier can also expected during the initial stages of interaction. Users may show some hesitation in using the technology. But in the long run a much more durable bond will develop.

Carefully planned video or audio packages may become extensions of their own story sharing experiences.

To begin with, audio cassettes seem to be the most promising and practical tool for the purpose. The possibilities are endless. Special effects, music, regional dealects can be used to design customized packages to maximise the effectiveness of the books.

This experiment should be conducted by choosing a few appropriate books and then translating them into audio cassettes. Most of the topics may be elaborated on audio cassettes for creating a better understanding of the written words.

Several course corrections may be required on the way to design an effective and user friendly package.

The usage of such audio cassettes in adult education libraries seems to be the fastest and most practical way to bring electronic media into action.

Although these audio cassettes can be produced easily and may prove very effective also, but their potential and reach is some what limited and incomplete. Complimentary video cassettes can definitely add unparalleled new dimensions to the print material. The effectiveness of such packages will be much greater than similar audio packages.

The existing cost structure for producing video software is prohibitive for a wide spread application of this technology for our purposes.

Lower cost alternatives must be explored to take advantage of this technology. Video software may be produced on VHS format at fraction of the cost of conventional u-matic format.

This approach may bring the electronic media into the adult education libraries.

Adult education libraries of future will have to experiment with different modes of electronic media to establish cost effective and meaningful learning modules to sustain and even accelerate the social revolution. Relevant governmental agencies and institutions like NIAE should take a serious look at this matter and launch a campaign to create audio/video software for adult education libraries.

The electronic media is here to stay. It reach and effectiveness is enormous. Delaying or postponing its application is only going to hurt the cause.

We must start using the electronic media in a big way in the adult education system and let technology set as a catalyst for the social change.

5

ROLE OF PUBLIC LIBRARIES IN THE PROMOTION OF POST-LITERACY AND CONTINUING EDUCATION

Dr. B.P. Barua

INTRODUCTION

Library service is an essential component of any programme of education-formal, non-formal and adult. The basic objective of all educational planning and organisations is to provide adequate scope to the people for the acquisition of knowledge with a view to improving their material and mental standards. Knowledge is vast and over expanding. It is recorded mainly in the shape of printed documents though there are other forms of storage such as discs, tapes, microfilms, microfiches etc. Libraries serve as the storehouses of knowledge. Easy access to the libraries is, therefore, essential for the progress of the individual and the nation.

While the importance of library service has been recognised for higher education and research, the same consciousness is not visible for general and mass education in all parts of the country. Thus, we have on the one hand developed university and college libraries, science and research libraries, but underdeveloped school and public libraries on the other. It is the public library which is relevant for the purpose of post-literacy and continuing education.

PUBLIC LIBRARY OBJECTIVES

A public library has been defined as a library which is maintained wholly out of public funds and which provides free service to the people regardless of race, colour, nationality, age, sex, religion, language, status or education attainment. The purpose of public library service has been aptly described by the UNESCO in its Manifesto.

"The public library is a practical demonstration of democracy's faith in universal education as a continuing and life long process, in the application of the achievement of humanity in knowledge and culture.

"It is the principal means whereby the record of man's thought and ideas and the expression of his creative imagination are made freely available to all.

"It is concerned with the refreshment of man's spirit with the provision of books for relaxation and pleasure".

Thus, public library has been visualised as an institution for lifelong and continuing education. It is expected to support not only formal education but also non-formal and general education of a people. Secondly, it is to serve as a centre for storing, retrieving and disseminationg information or knowledge. The public are to be kept informed about political, economic, social and cultural developments inside and outside the country in order that the enlightened public opinion help the national Government in taking correct decisions. Thirdly, a public library is an institution for promoting culture of the community. It has to organise cultural activities and to provide is to serce as the cultural nerve centre of the community. The last but not the least important function of a public library particularly in a developing country, is to promote adult education among the people.

PUBLIC LIBRARY ORGANISATION IN INDIA

The public library is the right institution for promoting post-literacy and continuing education in the country. Before the specific role of a public library in this sector is diescussed it is necessary to have some idea about the public library situation in the contry. The picture is not uniform. Under the constitution libraries, museums and other similar institutions except those declared under law as institutions of national importance form part of the State subjects. Though education, including technical education, medical institutions and universities has been transferred from the State list to the concurrent list by the 42nd amendment, the libraries and museums have continued to remain under the State list. Adult Education forming part of general education may be regarded as falling under the concurrent list. As the situation stands today, the Central Government can enact ligislation for promoting adult education, it cannot do so for promoting public library service.

The UNESCO has recommended that the public libraries "should be established under the clear mandate of law, so framed as to ensure nationwide provision of public library service" in order to build up a system of organised co-operation between libraries so that the total national resources can be fully utilised and palced at the service of a reader. The Advisory Committee for Libraries set up by the Ministry of Education, Government of India in its Report submitted to the Government in 1958 also reocmmended the adoption of library legislation by the States. A Model Public Libraries Bill was circulated among the States. Only eight States have so far adopted library legislation viz. Tamil nadu (1948), Andhra Pradesh (1960), Karnataka (1965), Maharashtra (1967). Of these the last three have not yet come into force. Generally speaking, the smaller States and Union Territories tend to develop library service by Governmental measures and the bigger States encourage the voluntary organisations to run the services. The general pattern is, however, to promote public library service partly by public effort and partly by private initiative with difference of degrees. Whatever may be the system of management and the procedure of financing, the quality of library service depends on the volume of input or the availability of resources for running the service in an adequate and efficient manner. Again, library service flourishes in places where reading habit is developed. Considering all these factors we may say that Tamil Nadu, Andhra Pradesh, Karnataka, Kerala, Maharashtra, Gujarat and West Bengal are more advanced in public library service than other states leaving aside the Union Territories of Delhi, Chandigarh and Pondicherry.

RURAL LIBRARY SITUATION IN INDIA

Since most of our illiterate people live in the villages the condition of rural libraries in different parts of the country deserves special study in the context of adult education programme and the role expected to be palyed by these libraries.

(1) Tamilnadu, Andhra Pradesh and Karnataka

These States have adopted library legislation with provision for library cess and set up autonomous Local or District Library Authorities. The District Library Authorities, on their part, have established Branch Libraries in the urban and rural areas of the districts. Thus a Branch Library may be found at a Taluka centre, a Panchayat Centre or a rural centre having five thousand population or so. The Branch Libraries form part of the district library system. A Branch Library on its turn may establish a Book Delivery Station at a smaller centre, usually in a school paying a nominal honorarium to a school teacher. The Union Territory of Pondicherry is also influenced by these States. They have decided to set up Mandal Libraries if there is no Branch Library existing in the Mandal

(2) Maharashtra and West Bengal

These two States have also adopted library legislation, but without the provision of library cess. Both the States encourage the development of library service by private initiative, through a planned operation of the grant-in-aid system. However, there are many State financed and sponsored town and rural libraries in West Bengal which form a class by themselves. The recognised public libraries of Maharashtra may be regarded as aided libraries. In both the States library service has spread to the block panchayat level except in a few places. Whether sponsored or aided by the Government, the condition of rural libraries in Maharashtra and West Bengal is better than many other States due mainly to the patronisation of the educated middle class.

(3) Kerala and Gujarat

In Kerala and Gujarat too library service has been developed by private initiative. The State Governments support their urban and rural libraries by an elaborate system of grant-in-aid to different categories of libraries. Library service has spread to the villages having a population of 5000 with the exception a few areas.

(4) Assam, Jammu & Kashmir, Tripura, Arunachal Pradesh and Mizoram

In these State, Governments have taken responsibility for establishing and developing libraries. The network of libraries has spread to the Sub-Division or Tehsil level. Library service at Block and Panchayat level are being developed through voluntary organisation. In view of smallness of the administrative units library coverage may be said to have reached the rural centres having 10000 to 20000 population.

(5) Rajasthan, Punjab and Haryana

In these States too the Governments are taking initiative to promote public library services. But the progress is somewhat slow and the coverage has remained limited to the district headquarters and municipal centres.

(6) Bihar, Madhya Pradesh and Uttar Pradesh

Library service is weakest in these States where even the district level libraries are not properly equipped to render the service. Though the number of libraries are many, these are mere excuses of libraries without the basic minimum standards of accommodation, staff and service. The Union Territory of Lakshadweep may be groupped in this category.

(7) Delhi, Chandigarh and Pondicherry

The Union Territories of Delhi, Chandigarh and Pondicherry are rather city States having high percentage of literacy. Delhi is covered by the network of libraries provided by Delhi Public Library. Chandigarh is well served by T.S. Central State Library, and Pondicherry, by Romain Rolland Library.

With so much diversity in the organisation of library services and the extent of illiteracy in the country, particularly at the rural level, it is impossible to visualise a single or uniform strategy for post-literacy, and continuing education.

Where library service has not reached the rural areas circulating library service should be organised among rural youth clubs from the District, Tehsil, Sub-Divisional and Taluka Library as the case may be. Wherever library service has spread to the villages, door to door library service should be developed with the help of social service and adult education workers and volunteers.

ADULT EDUCATION AND PUBLIC LIBRARY SERVICE

Adult education and public library service have identity of aims. Ignorance is sought to be removed from an illiterate person by giving him training in functional literacy so that he can expand his knowledge and better his lot by a process of lifelong and continuing education. The purpose of public library service is also the same. It provides education, information and recreation to the public for a better and fuller life. Both are complementary. Where adult education ends, public library service begins. In a broader context, adult education signifies lifelong education which is sought to be promoted by public library service as well.

There is thus unity of purpose between adult education and public library service. The goal is community development through community education. It is this concept which was embodied in the programme of social education adopted during the First Five Year Plan. Social Education included public libraries; it still does so in some State. The Advisory Committee on Libraries appointed by the Ministry of Education, Government of India recommended in its report submitted to the government in 1958 that an independent Directorate of Social Education and Libraries be created and, if that is not possible, a senior offer of the Education Department be placed in charge of the service. The close relationship between social education and library service was obviously realised. But then the concept has undergone metamorphosis. social education has yielded palce to adult education with emphasis on functional literacy. On the other hand, public libraries have been totally separated from adult education, and both are considered to be two distinct areas of operation and service. In fact there is no coordination among adult education, school education and public library service at the Central, State, District and village levels. But co-operation among the three units is necessary for the effective utilisation of limited resources and for rendering better service to the people.

FOLLOW-UP ACTION BY ADULT EDUCATION CENTRES

It is in the fitness of things that public libraries have not been entrusted with any responsibility for the first phase of the adult education programme or for literacy training though there is some clamour for this. A librarian remains busy in the evening hours and cannot afford to spare time for holding literacy class. At best a public library can provide space, if available, for running literacy classes. A public library may not also be immediately used for the follow-up programme leading to the reinforcemtn of the skill of literacy and numeracy and the prevention of relapse into illiteracy. This programme of limited objectives can be organised by the Adult Education Centres or the Continuing Education Centres or Jana Shiksha Nilayams as envisaged under the National Adult Education Programme. These centres are expected to make the learners self-reliant not only in reading and writing but also in understanding problems and finding their solutions. Once a person has developed autonomy in reading and understanding a subject, he is expected to use more and more reading materials to quench his newly acquired thirst for knowledge. It is at this state of post-literacy and continuing education that a public library becomes very much relevant.

LITERATURE FOR NEO-LITERATES

The production of suitable literature for the people with limited education assumes special importance at this stage. National Book Trust, Sahitya Akademi, Granth Academies, Adult Education Resource Centres and private publishers may be urged to produce suitable literature for this grup of readers. Annotated bibliographies of the available reading and other audio-visual materials may be prepared by Adult Education Directorates and ciruclated to the proper quarters to facilitate their acquisition. Vernacular newspapers, popular magazines, story books and fiction are the principal attractions for the common readers. The urban and rural public libraries are expected to stock these materials in adequate numbers for the use of their new clientele.

Of all the reading materials the role of a local vernacular newspaper is very significant. Common people are more interested in local news, local problems and local politics. Sports and pastimes. trade and commerce, agriculture and industries, transport and communication, education and helath and other important political and social developments of the region and the country would be the areas of interest for them. Although State-level vernacular newspapers are playing vital roles in popularising reading habit, they do not often reach the remote areas or neo-literates. This gap can be filled by a local newspaper. An Adult Education Centre or Continuing Education Centre located in Block headquarters would be the suitable agency for bringing out the newspaper. It may be produced in the shape of one sheet daily or two sheet weekly paper with a manually operated duplicating machine. The paper should be distributed free, if possible, or with nominal charge to meet the cost of distribution through a hawker. Such a paper will be immensely useful not only in sustaining literacy of the neo-literates but also in developing reading habit among the masses.

PUBLIC LIBRARIES AS COMMUNITY CENTRES

An effective way of drawing the new literates to the libraries is to organise the libraries as community or cultural centres. A library should serve as a meeting place of the community for cultural activities. In fact an ideal public library should have a small auditorium for cultural and audio-visual programmes. for holding meetings and talks, staging dramas, screening film shows, listening records, casettes and radio programmes, viewing television programmes, displaying charts and publicity materials of development departments and organising book exhibitions. Once people have been drawn to the library and their interests on certain topics have been aroused, suitable reading materials may be served to them.

People with limited education or neo-literates are hesitant to visit the libraries out of the sense of inferiority complex. The library and adult education workers will have to make special efforts to break their mental barriers and to draw them to library premises.

MOBILE AND CIRCULATING LIBRARY SERVICE

Steps should also be taken to deliver the books at the doorsteps of the new learners. In fact every established public library should organise mobile library service by means of cheap modes of transport or with the help of volunteers. The mobile or circulating library service may be organised in several forms suited to local circumstances (1) A library may develop book delivery stations or book deposit cintres in surrounding villages or localities, among youth clubs, primary schools etc., and books in batches may be circulated from one delivery station to another, (b) A bell cycle library service may be organised for delivering books at different village centres according to a scheduled programme. A rickshaw van may be used as a substitute, (c) If resources permit, a mechanised vehicle will be useful in a city or urban centre, (d) Door to door service may be organised for the handicapped persons with the help of volunteers and social service workers. Reaching the outreached should be the aim of all library centres.

CO-OPERATION AMONG DIFFERENT AGENCIES

Organisation of comprehensive library service requires adequate resources which are not available at present even for the district level public libraries. Similarly it may not be possible for the adult education organisers to find sufficienct resource for building up separate and permanent organisationa for post-literacy and continuing education programmes. A weak organisation tends to decline after the initial fervour is lost leading to stagnation and wastage. All the governmental agencies engaged in mass education should therefore pool their resources and coordinate their programmes for rendering better and lasting service to the people. The agencies which can fruitfully co-operate are:

(1) Secondary and Primary Education, Adult Education and Public Libraries. The school authorities can provide the space, the library authorities may supply the reading materials and the adult education authorities may provide the workers for bringing the books and the learners in contact with each other.

(2) Public Libraries, Adult Education, Health and Social Welfare. This will facilitate service to the handicapped persons.

(3) Public Libraries, Adult Education, Youth Services, Cultural Affairs and Information. This will promote community participation and cultural development.

(4) Public Libraries, Adult Education, Agriculture, Industries, Co-operation, Banking, Insurance, Employment and other economic and development agencies. Information generated by these departments may be gathered, stored and disseminated by the public libraries.

In all these spheres the role of libraries should be collection, storage and dissemination of information and the role of adult education workers should be mobilisation and organisation of the people for receiving the message delivered the different agencies of the Government for their welfare.

CONCLUSION

In these days of economic hardship and resource constraints there is no alternative but meaningful co-operation and sharing of responsibilities among different agancies engaged in social welfare activities.

6

ROLE OF LIBRARY IN ADULT EDUCATION

Prof. S. Ansari

It is no more a most point that "education can no longer follow the path blazed for it by age-old tradition. Systems and practices which restrict men's education to childhood and youth and which perpetuate the objectives and methods of our fore fathers without reference to the way in which people really live or to the diversity of human nature are providing more and more to be erroneous, ineffective and unjust. The research and thinking of psychologists, sociologists and economists and the experience of more perceptive educators lead to the same conclusion, namely that education must be considered as a continuous process going on through out one's life and every stage of one's development".

The move for adult education initiated in the middle of the 19th century was only a partial realisation of the above facts regarding human needs that had become sharp in the context of the emerging industrial society. A new class of industrial workforce was now coming face to face with a situation in which on the one side limitless opportunities for betterment of life were becoming available and on the other, he was finding himself handicapped in obtaining the benefits for himself due to missed educational opportunities. Adult education was therefore, at this stage equated with education for workmen. A mixed motive to attain better condition of living; to satisfy a desire for knowledge and understanding or and to acquire competitive weapons promted them to join eveing classes that were organised by voluntary institutions.

However, the pattern of education evolved for adults at this stage was modelled on the traditional pattern of instruction: One-way transmittal of knowledge, excercises, tasks, checking of learing acquired, examination and diplomas. However, this was supported by libraries set up by voluntary organisations as well as those run on subscriptions. We have good example of such support in efforts made by Carnegi Corporation both in US and UK.

The society has now moved away from industrial to information society. In an information society the axial principle of development is the central place for theoretical knowledge and information, which is source of innovation, policy formulation and of executive function. Some of the characteristics of the new society are:

i) A change from goods producing to a service society.
ii) Increasing effort for codification of theoretical knowledge necessary for innovation.
iii) The creation of a intellectual technology as a key tool for generation of wealth.

The changing dimension has led to a revolt against the traditional pattern of adult education. From being subjected to educationan adult has now become himself an instrument of his own education. This new individual is "endowed with his own psychological and sociological options, aware of his own individuality, and is engaged in a series of contests, each having its particular objective: the contest for survival, the contest for knowledge, the contest for individual and collective advancement. This new adult is driven to education, not under compulsion as a student, but by self-interest. Unless he perceives any link between what is offered to him and his own ambitions, hopes, inquisitiveness, and tastes, he remains aloof from facilities for education extended to him.

CHANGING CONCEPT OF ADULT EDUCATION

In a world moving from authoritarian or one-party political system to a multi-party democratic system the adult has acquired a new role, the role of taking informed decisions in electing a government. Freedom to choose is based on the need to understand the meaing of democracy and the issues on which elections will be contested. Adult education therefore now becomes a useful instrument in shaping the minds of the people and enabling him to function effectively in democracy.

The new task of the adult education is therefore, to provide individual with knowledge essential for performance of his economic, social and political function in a democratic set up and especially to enable them through participation in the life of their communities to live fuller and more harmonious life. Accordingly, the aim of adult education has become to ensure training and not instruction: it seeks to create an atmosphere of intellectual curiosity, social freedom and tolerance, and to stimulate in each person the demand and the capacity to take part in the development of cultural life of his day.

In the coming years, the desire to tolerate differences of opinion and to have respect for divergent views will be the determining factor for the success of a multi-party democracy.

MODES OF ADULT EDUCATION

Adult education may be grouped under three modes: Education for adults outside the formal system not leading to qualification; education for adults outside the formal system leading to qualification; deliberate provision for adult within the formal system.

ADULT EDUCATION AND LITERACY

While it is important not to make mistake of treating adult education as the same as literacy work, in a country like India where illiteracy has been increasing in absolute term, any programme of adult education has to take into consideration the existing situation of literacy. The document National Policy on Education, 1986: Programme of Action has identified the following situation regarding literacy.

i) Illiteracy has increased in absolute terms.

ii) The situation is pretty bad in female and SC/ST sector.
iii) Misuse of literacy resulting into relapse to illiteracy.
iv) Scanty opportunity for continuing education.
v) Scanty opportunity for access to information.
vi) Science, technology and modern research have not been applied to literacy programmes.
vii) Youths, workers and masses have remained involved.

ROLE OF LIBRARIES

The aims and objectives of adult education the curriculum, the instruction method, all have been discussed and analysed thread bare by experts. However, the one thing, central in importance for the success of any programme of education that has remained neglected, more so in our country is the place of Library. The negligence is not so much on the part of realisation of pivotal role of Library as it is on the part of provision for Library system. The document cited above has emphasised the role of Library in the following words.

ROLE OF LIBRARY

(1) Continuing education, Establishment of Jana Shikshan Nilayams for clusters of villages which will provide facilities for Library reading room, Charchamandal, Cultural Activities and may also include a Community TV set.

(4) Programmes of book promotion will be taken up on the lines indicated in the Policy, Libraries and Reading rooms in educational institutions will be opened to the public in the evenings and necessary additional grants provided to them for the purpose. Voluntary efforts for establishment of reading rooms and Libraries will be encouraged.

Similarly, the document entitled National Policy on Education, 1986, after emphasising the place of literacy for producting manpower resources needed for a developing country the policy frame spells out ways and channels through which a vast programme of adult and continuing education will be implemented. One component of the programme is wider promotion of books, Libraries and reading rooms.

Again in part VIII of the document *Re-orienting the content and process of education*, under section Books & Libraries, the policy document talks of measures "to improve the quality of books, promote the reading habit, and encourage quality writing". Together with the development of books, a nation wide movement for the improvement of existing libraries and the establishment of new ones will be taken up. Provision will be made in all educational institutions for library facilities and the status of librarians improved.

Most of the studies carried out by researchers or Government appointed Committees have underlined the role that public library can play in promoting adult education. As far back as in 1958, the Sinha Committee recommended that "Libraries should interact with other social education and adult education programme". The Committee recommended establishment of libraries for the purpose at Block, District and State levels. This recommendation was in line with the UNESCO concept of a "public Library as a living force of popular education".

The recommendation however after more than three decades is yet to be fully implemented as will be obvious from the present state of public libraries in the country.

Type of Library	Number of Libraries
State Central Library	15 (as against 22 States)
Union Territories	4 (as against 9 Territories)
District Central Library	291 (as against 402 Districts)
Block Library	1798 (as against 5027 Blocks)
Village Library	41828 (as against 5,75,936 Villages)

LIBRARY LEGISLATION

Central	Not yet
Stage Level	10 States
Union Territories	Not Yet

A comparison of the state of public Library in India with the UK and USA presents a dismal picture for our country.

Item	India	UK.	U.S.A.
Population	100 million (post 1971 census)	55 million (1971)	159 million (1967)
Literacy	36%(1980)	100%	99%
Total expenditure on education p.a.	Rs. 11,000 million (1971-72)	Rs. 8,739 million (1970-71)	Rs. 38,33,700 million (1970)
Annual expenditure on Public Libraries	53,554 (1973)	11,500 (1969)	10,459 (1966-67)
Book stock per 100 person	1 (1965)	145 (1965)	100 (1965)

In addition to inadeqate expansion in public Library system, there appears to be lack of co-ordination so essential for proper utilisation of limited resources. Thus, it would have saved much resources if instead of stocking books at Jana Shikshan Nilayam, the resources of Panchayat and Block Libraries were augmented and these libraries were involved in adult education progremme. In this connection the following recommendation of a National Seminar on Public Library Movement organised by the Raja Ram Mohun Roy Library Foundation in Tamil Nadu, in April 1991, is very relevant.

> "In view of the fact that measures initiated by the Government for eradication of illiteracy in the country have not yielded the desired results owing to the absence of well organised public library services to sustain literacy, it is recommended that the Government of India should set apart a sizeable portion of money ear-marked for national literacy mission for improving public library services through out the country. The establishment of Jana Shikshan Nilayams as a parallel Library system for neo-literates can only lead to wasteful duplication and drain of meagre resources".

The seminar further recommended that the public Library system should be entrusted with the responsibility of catering to the needs of neo-literates at least in those States with a public Library Act.

Establishment of Jana Shikshan Nilayams all over the country was started in a phased manner in 1988. Authorities are stocking them with huge supply of books without knowing abilities and interests of neo-literates. There is a general impression that people like to read books on religion, books that may help them in their profession and so on. A recent survey conducted in Cuddapah district in A.P. has revealed the following ranking of preference.

Items of reading	**Ranking**
Newspaper	1
Cine Magazine	2
Novels	3
Balmitra, Chandamama	4
Books on Health	5
Books on history of national leaders	6.5
Song books	10.5
Books on occupation	12
Book on mythology	13.5

The above is by no means a representative picture. But it does underline one thing: the books stocked in a library should be selected keeping in view the user's need and interest area.

The role of academic libraries is no less important in promotion of adult education. The authorities such as the UGC have already realised the value of net-working the resources of University and research institution libraries for their fuller utilisation. The academic libraries can meet the information and library needs of the higher and of technical stream adult educands. Even the resources of the Block and village level libraries can be augmented through extension service. In fact the Directorate of Extension Service in the Karnataka University has, since its inception organised, and been running a circulating library system in the rural areas. The Jamia Milia

Islamia also had organised extension work through its Urdu Centres in various parts of Delhi.

The concept of adult education has ceased to be a one step effort for making up for the missed opportunities. It is now replaced by life long learning. Preparation of suitable literature, designing proper curriculum, adopting new techniques of imparting training and instruction and utilisation of mass media as means for communication, all have their place in any scheme for adult education. But without proper library support there is little chance of sustaining the programme. The country needs a well knit library system. But to bring about a system the country must formulate its national policy on library and information system. It is the Government placed before the Parliament the recommendations of the Empowered Committee on National Policy on Library and Information System. Similarly, steps should be taken to enact Library legislation in all the states and Union Territories so that proper financial and legal support is available in the country for Public Library System.

7

ROLE OF LIBRARIES IN THE ADULT EDUCATION IN RURAL AND TRIBAL AREAS

Prof. Nanubhai N. Joshi

South Gujarat University-Surat commands, Surat, Bharuch, Valsad, and Dang District which are thickly populated with tribal population. Dharmpur taluka of Valsad district is the biggest taluka of India as per the area is concerned (i.e. 238 villages spread over 1650 sq. km). Majority of the tribals live in the forest areas the advancement of science and technology along with the spread of Adult Education should be made available to them so that it should become a tool to improve their life, take them out from the blind beliefs and make them active participants in the provcess of their development.

Libraries can play a very effective role in the eradication of illiteracy. Libraries are instruments of non-formal education of illiteracy, and adult education is nothing else but non-formal education. The libraries cannot help only the teacher (whosoever he may be) in the eradication of illiteracy but can help him in consolidation of his gains by preventing the neo literate from sliding back into illiteracy. Not only this, libraries can support the neo literate in further self-education and enable him to reap the fruits of literacy. In a way libraries can act 'after-care-house' for those who pass out from the adult literacy school.

Libraries can help the campaign in the following manner:-

1. Half of literacy-teacher's battle is won if the illiterate develop a will to become literate. The libraries equipped

with audiovisual aids can carry on successful motivation through charts, picture, films and television shows and through various socal education activities.

2. They can prepare annotated bibliographies for all grades of pupils and organise book exhibitions and thus help the teacher's selection of the right type of reading materials for all levels of his pupils.
3. They can select, stock and serve easy to read material for the actual work of literacy, and serve the following reading material to those who have picked up functional literacy.
4. Supply the teacher and organisers of the literacy campaign with books on latest techniques and reports on researches, methods and policies. It can prevent the teacher's own knowledge and techniques from going stale.
5. Surveys of the reading interests of the new literate to cultivate the habit of reading at public library in rural areas. It can help in the production of literature suited to the reader's needs.

In our country there is an independent of adult education. Any educational endeavour has to base on the backing of good library. Whatever in education is planned or contemplated to be done, the first requirement is a good library. A library cannot be built overnight, good libraries are built constant hard work performed with dedication. Our adult educational programme, unfortunately is not having backing of a good library system. Quantitatively we may be satisfied with figures of progress. However, much is left to be desired as far as quality is concerned. If this programme is backed by a network of libraries, the results will be many time more impressive and progress amazing.

The field of adult education activities is a product of the cultural process of the various groups. The communities differ in outlook and character. It is but natural that these activities also differ accordingly. In view of Indian requirements, the following activities will have to be added to the last group of activities.

1. Promotion of literacy 2. Providing recreational facilities 3. Organizing study groups secular or religious 4. Holding poetical symposia etc. 5. Arranging radio programs. 6. Organising kirtan and kathas 7. Holding competitions on all types of activities conducted. 8. Teaching good hobbies. 9. Imparting vocational training 10. Working with other institutions in various fiedls to enlist their support for library programmes.

The adult education activities being carried out by libraries in different countries successfully give a new meaning to adult education.

Here the libraries stepped in and gave the highest dignity to the individual by paying special attention to his specific needs operating on an informal basis. They moved beyond the functions of furnishing materials and information to that of advising adults on reading and study programmes planned to meet the individual's needs at his own reading level and on his own time. They went ahead further with a robust confidence. These liberal activities are described by presenting typical cases wherever possible.

The existing public libraries have to play role with dedication because the role of library as a social education agency is unique. With a varied book stock, it can appeal to all ages, class and occupations. Its offerings are never forced and, therefore, and the more readily acceptable. Above all it is an agency for continued education. The library, therefore, has to be active and positive in its policy and a dynamic part of community life. For these new avenues have to be opened new ways have to be found and tried out. To make the library an effective instrument of community development. We have to apply ourselves to this challenging task more vigorously and more imaginatively with a complete devotion to this nobel cause.

Library service has three distinct roles in the field of adult education. First as a supplementary aid to other agencies, then as an independent agency and lastly as a stimulating and motivating force taking a leadership role. Adult education is now a central theme of library service and is one of the many off-shoots of personal assistance to readers. Motivation is as necessary as other two roles. Adults are engaged in their main programmes and there are many other demands of their priorities. Our success is in proportion to our ability to get them interested in our programmes. We have to create an adult education explosion and then to harness the energy released by it for further development of our human resources. The areas of greatest development are amongst women, people in early retirement and young adults and these areas must be planned for.

The illiterate who consist of about 70% population of the country are proving a challenge to adult educators and the librarians. Their education is as important as that of literate members of the community. Funds for the maintenence, expansion of public libraries are provided not only literate members of the community but by the illiterates as well. They are also paying taxes and provide money for libraries. Thus why they should be denied to use it? In fairness to illiterates the adult educators and the libraries should have substaintial programmes for them.

The problem of providing education facilities to adult illiterates is so great and complex it can not considered independently either of adult educators or of librarians. They should join their hands and work together to meet the needs of adult illiterates. The job of adult education should be to explore the field, prepare the ground of willingness and readyness for learning and the function of librarians should be to provide the tools of self-education, development and familiarise the community with opportunity which can be avail in the life.

The summrise the above thoughts the prime important work of libraries is—

1. to provide reading facilities to the neo literate at their door steps by arranging for mobile library.

2. The village should be provided with village library as a part of district panchayat Programme or Jana Shikshan Nilayam.
3. Mobile libraries can be organised either by mobile library van or on cycle.

The Department of Continuing Education and Extension work of South Gujarat University, Surat has established 13 Block of Surat district. This library will cater to the needs of neoliterate and villagers at large. It will also spread the Gandhian philosophy among the readers. The library expenses will be borne by the voluntary association. The department under its continuing education programme provides training facilities to the village school teachers who can look after the village library. The training course content includes title, selection of books, library adminstration, classification system, card system etc.

The Department organised literacy centres in Dang and Dharampur taluka for illiterate adults where sixty centres were organised. Huge number of neo literates are served with library facilities through JSN scheme.

8

READING MATERIAL FOR NEO-LITERATES

Varsha Das

The books for neo-literates in various Indian languages are needed urgently and in huge quantities, more than even before. Thanks to the literacy campaigns all over the country. This need has given new challenges to writers and publishers because a new form of writing has emerged which is different from what we have for educated adults and children.

Neo-literates are that class of readers who have rich vocabulary for their day to day dealings, who have indigenous technical terminology connected with their specific vocation, who have a valuable treasure of oral literary traditions but who lag behind in the efficient and independent use of the skills of reading, writing and arithmatic.

Before 1988, post-literacy training was centre based. It was, therefore, guided learning and was also monitored. But after the establishment of Jana Shikshan Nilayams it is now a voluntary effort on the part of the neo-literates. These JSNs are basically continuing education centres having a reading room and a library. The neo-literates are expected to go to then Jana Shikshan Nilayams, pick up the book and read for retaining and stabilizing the reading skill achieved in the basic literacy class. Reading for recreation is not expected from all the neo-literates. The Prerak, the person in charge of the Jana Shikshan Nilayam is supposed to play the role of the friend, philosophar and guide in the post-literacy phase of neo-literates.

Before we discuss the nature of books for neo-literates, it is important to look into the levels of their literacy skills. The neo-literates who have acquired the basic skills of 3Rs through primary education or through literacy classes can be classified into three categories.

1. **Beginning Level:** These neo-literates need guidance to use learning material. They require simple and interesting text suited to their reading ability.
2. **Middle Level:** The Neo-literates of this category can read interesting stories, newspapers and they try to understand them in relation to their daily experiences.
3. **Self-learning Level:** This group of neo-literates can read books and newspapers independently. They are willing to go to the libraries and other places for reading materials. They are also motivated to join formal education system for a degree or certificate.

The reading material should be such that the reader can strengthen, stabilise and apply literacy skills. Adult learning is a complex process. Human mind is vulnerable. The writer has to give confidence to the reader that he or she can read, and that learing can be life long for better quality of life. Some doubts are raised regarding the learning capacity of an adult. As early as in 1927, a well-known psychologist Edward L. Thorndike had found through his studies that the ability to learn declines only very slowly and very slightly (i.e., one percent per year) after the age of 20. This decline is also only in the speed of learning, not of the intellectual power. Learning ability actually can be improved through better learning environment, better teaching methods and better learning materials. An adult cannot be forced to study a particular learning materials. Motivating them for further learning becomes difficult only in the absence of literacy environment.

Neo-literate materials, therefore, should be suited to learning skills, should focus on real and immediate problems of the readers, should promote active learning which would help the reader to develop a critical attitude towards problems, reflect on them, analyse, discuss and take action. We can also have special type of materials for special groups like for women, for minority communities, for immigrants, tribals etc.

The content of these materials should be co-related with individual and social development goals. They should have ideas and information. Information is not just passed in, but should pose potential problems and conditions, and provide related knowledge to help solve the problem. Writers can use the rich material already available in the fold literature, cultural heritage, day to day experience of readers etc. It is important to give the text which can be easily read and understood.

The language should be the language of the region, simple, attractive, interesting and suited to their level of maturity. Adult learners should not be treated like children. According to a number of guidelines and also may own experience, it has been found that short sentences of 6-8 words, avoiding conjunct letters atleast in the first 6-7 pages, having small paragraphs of about 7-8 lines, small chapters of 2-3 pages and using clear type face in 18-20 pts. helps the reader to read fast and in the process develops confidence regarding his or her reading skills.

Libraries can use visual aids like charts, drawings, photographs etc. to create literacy environment and provide visual aids.

The best method of preparing the manuscript can be as follows :

1. **Survey:** The knowledge of readers profile and socio-economic condition would help the writer to create the text which would be closer to the life of the reader.
2. **Indentification of Topics:** The topic if relevant to the reader has more chances of attracting the readers. At times certain incidents or personalities from the past or the present can also be appealing for the reader.
3. **Selection of Format:** Depending upon the topic and the reading ability of the reader, the writer can decide the format of the book, i.e., whether printed book or printed

non-book, whether a story or a straight narration, whether heavily illustrated or less illustrations etc.

The text will be highly improved if it is field tested. There are two methods of field testing. One, to enlarge the type script on a photocopier or write the whole text in big and legible hand and take it to a group of neo-literates to make them read. This exercise requires the presence of the writer, illustrator and adult education functionaries of that area in whose presence the reader would be relaxed. Another method is to make a number of copies of the text and give the responsibility to an Adult Education Functionary to leave it with the neo-literates for a week or two and then go from person to person, check their difficult spots. In the National Book Trust, we are following the first method and we have fund it more useful and effective. It is also a kind of a training for the writer and the illustrator. The writers understand the literacy level, comprehension level and also the environment of the neo-literate through this kind of inter-action.

After the field testing, the manuscript is revised. Difficult words are substituted by the simple ones. Abstract or difficult concepts are dropped or substituted or elaborated by the writer. The manuscript is then finalised for production.

The illustrator's role is vital in preparing reading material for neo-literates. She has to be authentic and realistic in her approach. Field testing of illustrations also helps the illustrator to fill up the gap between the reader and the visual. Illustrations can be in 2 colours to cut down the printing cost.

There is a need for neoliterate material in all the languages all over the country. To prevent the relapse into illiteracy and by that saving the human and financial efforts from becoming futile let there be a flood of neo-literate material available in every village. This requires concerted efforts on the part of not only Adult Education functionaries but all of us, all who are interested in improving the quality of life in this very century.

LIBRARIES IN DISTANCE EDUCATION

Dr. Neela Jagannathan

The role of the library within any academic institution can be realised only in the context of the institutions philosophy of education. This is true of most of the libraries of the world's academic institutions in general and libraries of open universities in particular. This statement can be examined by taking a concrete example of the Indira Gandhi National Open University rather than discussing in abstract terms.

The main objectives of IGNOU are to advance and disseminate learning and knowledge by a diversity of means, including the use of modern communication technology and providing opportunities for higher education to masses residing in remote and rural areas. It aims at encouraging the open education and correspondence education throughout the country; it also seeks to co-ordinate and determine the standards of teaching-learning process through distance education in other open universities of India. The Library and Documentation Division being a part of IGNOU's organisational structure, the objectives of the library have to match with those of the IGNOU. The basic objectives of the library are—

* to develop appropriate collecion in various disciplines for satisfying the needs of the diverse clientele of the libraries of the main University, Regional and Study Centres;
* to provide reading, lending, reference information and documentation facilities to all categories of staff and students;

* to develop special collection of distance education books and journals at the libraries of the Headquarters as well as Regional Centres;
* to provide documentation and comprehensive reference/ information services in areas related to distance education to other open universities of the world in general and India in particular.

IGNOU library strives hard to fulfil these objectives inspits of several constraints such as lack of adequate space, staff and finance.

At this juncture, the topic "Role of Libraries in Adult Education" selected for the National Seminar by the National Institute of Adult Education during the important event of Tenth World Book Fair is highly relevant. It is a well known fact that most of the countries have facilities to impart higher education through correspondence and open universities. So, a large proportion of the adult population is pursuing their studies through distance education system. Their need for library services can neither be disputed nor denied.

NETWORK OF LIBRARIES AT OPEN UNIVERSITIES

Most of the distance teaching universities operate either through three-tier system consisting of the main university, Regional centres and study centres like the Indira Gandhi National Open University (IGNOU) and U.K. Open University or through two-tier system having the University Headquarters and Study Centres-namely Andhra Pradesh Open University (APOU) and Sukhothai Thammathirat Open University, Thailand, IGNOU & APOU have a network of libraries comprisin two distinct categories.

a) Central library as the apex at the University Headquarters,
b) Libraries at the Regional and Study Centres as the branch libraries.

The Central Library combines the features and functions of both, an academic library as well as a special library. This dual characteristic increases the complexity of library policies regarding the development of collection and provision of library and information services.

ACQUISITION MANAGEMENT

Acquisition management being a centralised process, the Central Library has the responsibility of building collection for the main as well as branch libraries. The process of selection and acquisition, the collection and its organisation and clientele vary a great deal from each other.

The selection of library materials is the joint responsibility of the librarian and the academic staff. Print and non-print materials such as books, periodicals, reports, recordings, films, slides, microforms, computer floppies, globes, models, dioramas, kits etc. are acquired to facilitate the production of multimedia packages of course materials. The Central Library caters to the requirements of academic and media consultants, professional, technical and administrative staff involved in the course development i.e. planning, designing, creating, producing and distributing of multi-media package.

The process of acquisition and organisation is centralised at the Central Library to have consistency and standardisation which may help in computerising house-keeping operations and networking of all types of libraries in the long run. Library acquires multiple copies of books for the Regional and Study Centes. They are selected by the academic staff of the various disciplines keeping in mind the availabity and readability of the books. They are selected according to the course requirements and levels of the target groups. As far as possible, books recommended by the course writers as 'Suggested Readings' at the end of each unit or block are acquired for Regional and Study Centres' Libraries. The books are processed i.e. accessioned, classified and catalogued at the Central Library before despatching them to the respective centres. The libraries of the Regional Centes are resource libraries to cater to the needs of academic and research scholars of the various academic institutions whereas the students and the part-time counsellors engaged to impart guidance to the learners in each discipline are the potential users of the core library at the Study Centre.

In order to satisfy the demands of the distance learners, librarians have to recognise the main characteristics of independent learners and identify their requirements.

CHARACTERISTICS OF DISTANCE LEARNERS

Distance learners are motivated, matured adults belonging to different socio-economic, cultural, educational and linguistic backgrounds. They widely vary in age, qualifications, objectives and interests. They may be employed, unemployed, retired, single, married, housewives, physically disabled having varied social and financial problems. Their learning activity being part-time in leisure hours, namely in the evenings and on holidays, they are flexible in their studies. They may either study individually at home, at work, in a library or in a group at the study centres while attending counselling and contact programmes. They differ in their methods of pursuing studies using various study skills, previous learning experience, fluency of expression and so on.

Apart from this, the courses undertaken by the learners may be either in routine and traditional subjects or be highly technical and professional or involve creative skills. They may be of varied levels ranging from elementary or introductory to advanced studies.

LIBRARY REQUIREMENTS OF DISTANCE LEARNERS

The library requirements of such varied sections of learner population can be grouped under three categories :

a) Need for materials and facilities
b) Need for information services
c) Need for user services

a) Need for materials and facilities:

Distance learners require access to library resources either for reference on premises or borrowing them for study at home or getting them on inter-library loan through the library. They need the following materials and facilities :

* Reference and textbooks
* Self-instructional materials and open packages developed by various distance teaching universities
* Audio-visual and non-print materials from various organisations
* Audio-video equipment and hardware, word processor or typewriter, photocopier/xerox machine, microfiche reader-cum-printer, computer, etc.
* Lecture or discussion room for the independent learners to meet and to hear/view audio-video programmes.

b) Need for Information Services:

If the distance learners are provided access to well-organised resources and facilities, there should be well-trained library staff to collect, process, organise, store and disseminate information to users. Even if the materials are not available at the library, the staff should be able to provide up-to-date information regarding—

* bibliographical information about reference sources, books, journals, non-print materials available at their own library or those which can be borrowed on inter-library loan from the other libraries
* information regarding self-instructional materials, multimedia materials, educational programmes of radio and television broadcasts
* information regarding various other organisations imparting education and training opportunities through distance mode and their courses
* information regarding Regional and Study Centres, their contact and counselling programmes, summer schools, laboratory and library facilities, special lectures, available resources and facilities etc.

c) Need for User Services

Adult, independent learners also need professional guidance and support from the library staff about :

* Using the library collection
* Using the available equipment and facilities at the library
* Selecting the reading materials
* Planning their learning
* Utilising the study skills for self-learning.

In order to fulfil these requirements, library staff should be willing to promote user education and information literacy. Librarian should arrange a lecture or present a self-instructional video show regarding the collection, its user and function, available equipment and facilities of the library. The services and holdings of the library should be publicised. In order to ensure the effective user of the library, they should provide printed information, library guides to the collection, posters, display of new additions, notices, rules and regulations, instructions, etc... They may arrange illustrated talks by the subject specialists to assist the distance learners in pursuing their studies.

LIBRARY & INFORMATION SERVICES TO DISTANCE LEARNERS

The provision of library and information services is as much of vital importance to the distance learners like their counterparts in conventional universities. Library policies of different distance teaching universities in India and aboard vary from zero provision of books to exhaustive library services. In India, there are more than 40 universities offering correspondence courses but their library services to external students are negligible whereas the library of University of South Africa promotes distance teaching by providing exhaustive library services. University of Manitoba in Canada, University of New England in New South Wales-Australia, Deakin University in Victoria-Australia,

University of the South Pacific in Suva, Fiji etc. offer regular and correspondence (distance education) courses and give a high priority to the provision of library services to both their on-campus and off-campus students. They have the same system of Central Library and Study Centres libraries as we have in Indian open universities, but their library services are much more functional because they lend books through postal/courier services and provide xerox copies of journal articles from the Central Library without any additional charges. In Thailand, students of the Sukhothai Thammathirat Open University do not have libraries at their study centres. They usually avail of library services at the nearby public libraries. The Public Libraries system is well organised in these countries and they have attained great popularity by promoting distance education and by providing library and information services to adult learners.

Unlike the libraries of the conventional universities which cater to a few hundreds of faculty members, research scholars, students and administrators in a particular city, the librarians of the distance teaching universities have to cater to the needs of thousands of distance learners of diverse categories scattered all over the country or state. Again, the Central Library at the headquarters faces the challenging task of acquisitions management and collection development for different categories of clientele, considering their requirements. They have not only to acquire, process, despatch and monitor the receipt of the books & non-print materials sent to the Centres but also to take policy decisions regarding the management of the branch libraries as well as providing the maximum services safeguarding the resources.

The librarians of both National as well as State Open Universities in India have been struggling hard to provide reading and reference services to their distance learners but they encounter enormous problems due to various constraints namely lack of infrastructural facilities at the centres, paucity of staff, limited finance, literature explosion, spiralling prices, complexity of demands from diverse users and so on.

Though adequate care is taken to make the specially designed self-instructional, multi-media packages self-contained, learners of the postgraduate degree and diploma programmes have to depend on some additional textbooks suggested at the end of each unit/block for writing the assignments and preparation for examinations.

The Regional and Study Centres housed in the existing colleges and educational institutions, do not have enough accomodation for library stackroom and reading room. Owing to lack of qualified, experienced and regular staff, proper information services are not provided. Circulation of books including issuing, adjustments of loans, reservation of books etc. is not possible as learners attendance at contact or counselling sessions is optional. So the books are issued for reference at the premises to prevent losses and ensure their availability to other students. The students residing in rural, remote geographical areas cannot avail the reading facilities or listening and watching to audio-video programmes at the Centre's library. Budgetary constraints are still graver. In a multilingual country like India, the learners of the different states expect the open university to supply course materials, reference books, textbooks and audio-video programmes in their own Regional languages whereas standard textbooks in science, technology, engineering etc. are not available even in Hindi leave aside the other Regional Languages.

In developing countries where modern sophisticated gadgets like TV, VCR, taperecorder, radio, telephone, computer etc. are not equally and adequately accessible to all the distance learners, library facilities have to remain one of the basic student support services to learners. Thus, libraries have to play a significant role to provide library and information services to the distance learners. But in Indian context this tremendous task of providing library facilities to masses scattered over the whole country cannot be accomplished by the distance teaching universities alone. They have to meet with the demands of the diverse learners by cooperating with all types of libraries, viz academic, learners by cooperating with all types of libraries, viz academic, special and public, to extend appropriate library service to the learners. This can be possible by the joint efforts of all the existing libraries and utilising their infrastructural facilities and library resources for longer hours which otherwise remain idle on the holidays and evenings, to cater to the needs of the distance learners without the imposition of additional financial burdem.

CONCLUSION

Let me conclude that there is no doubt about the saying charity begins at home. The beginning has to be made by the distance teaching institutions. The major responsibilities lie with the libraries of the various open universities to make this mission fruitful by gathering, processing, organising, storing and disseminating relevant information to all the existing libraries to provide effective and efficient services to the needy learners. Automation of library operations and networking of all types of libraries can facilitate in extending the library and information services to distance learners. The librarians have to make policy decisions regarding the maximum use of existing resources. They should compromise between the conflicting views of rendering services primarily to their own members but at the same time making the resources available also to the adult, matured students pursuing studies independently, by making appropriate arrangements for safeguarding the collection. The development of a network of public libraries in each state and establishing interstate linkages to form a national network will serve the potential group of distance learners along with the general public. No doubt, this may seem difficult in this era of financial constraints but it is not impossible. It presents a challenge to the librarians by attempting to change their traditional outlook and aim "towards the educational role of public libraries and the public role of academic libraries (Fisher-1988).

REFERENCES

1. Fisher, Raymond K. "Library Services for Adult Continuing Education and Independent Learning Guide London, Library Association, 1988.
2. Kaul, B.N. et.at., ed. - "Studies in Distance Education" New Delhi. AIU & IGNOU, 1988.
3. Neela Jagannathan - "Collection Development at Andhra Pradesh Open University Libraries" Library Acquisitions: Practice and Theory V. 12(3-4); 1988, pp. 281-296.
4. Neela Jagannathan - "Collection Development at the Libraries of Distance Teaching Universities with Special Reference to the Indian Situation" *ILA Bulletin,* XXII (3), Oct-Dec. 1987, pp. 140-148.
5. Neela Jagannathan "Role of Public Libraries in Distance Education in India" *In Libraries in Distance Education ed. by K.A. Isaac and G. Devarajan.* New Delhi: Ess Ess, 1989.
6. Neela Jaganathan- "Library Services to Distance Learners" *University News* XXVII(47); Nov. 20, 1989, pp. 8-13.
7. Perry, Walter- "Open Univesity: A Personal Account by the First Vice-Chancellor" Milton Keynes. Open University Press, 1976.
8. Ram Reddy, G.- Reading in Distance Education-I. New Delhi. IGNOU. 1987.

10

THE ROLE OF DELHI PUBLIC LIBRARY IN ADULT EDUCATION : A RECAPITULATION

D.R. Kalia

Delhi public Library was sponsored jointly by UNESCO and the Government of India, Ministry of Education in 1951as the first international Public library pilot project to demonstrate the potential of a public library service in continuing education. Never before an international organisation and a national government had cooperated in the setting up of a public library which hitherto was the preserve of a local government (municipalities and rural counties).

Its stimulating influence was intended to permeate the entire developing world and spawn similar projects in the other regions and countries as paragons. As a successful paradigm in Asia, two similar projects were established, one for Africa in East Nigeria and another for Latin America in Colombia. The nature and scope of services of the three projects were defined in the UNESCO Public Library Manifesto which inter alia laid down that a modern public library should function as a dynamic institution for the promotion of adult education for all classes of users, and not merely as a passive storehouse of books. It should provide reading material for the new reading public as well which comprised new literates and school dropouts.

In 1950s the rate of literacy in India was only 17% (male 25% and female 8%) and about 33% in Delhi. Adult education with emphasis on literacy started during the freedom movement spearheaded by Mahatma Gandhi in 1920s in which voluntary organisations played a major role. Government took this responsibility on to itself only after independence when separate departments of adult education were established in the States. The Central Government under the sponsorship of UNESCO, established the Insititute of Fundamental Education in New Delhi, to oversee the programme for spread of literacy and production of suitable reading material for the neo-literates. But by 1951 the fundamental education programme was in a fledgling stage. The Indian Adult Education Association. New Delhi was the national forum for the promotion of adult education through voluntary effort and government agencies. It held annual conferences and workshops all over the country. The Jamia Milia Islamia, New Delhi played a pioneering role in the production of reading material for the neo literates. The Delhi Municipality had a Department of Urban Community Development which organised literacy classes all over the city. Interchangeable, several terms were used over the years to express the scope of adult education, such as fundamental education, social education, community education and social service. Functional literacy constituted on important segment of all of them.

THE NEW READING PUBLIC

Delhi Public Library undertook a project to find out what material existed in Hindi and Urdu for the new reading public. The entire material available in these two languages was collected, and evaluated. it was found that there were good primers available and some material for post-literacy, but almost nothing for the new reading public whose ranks were swelling with the spread of literacy and the dropouts which constituted as high as 60% of the students enrolled in five year primary schools. Several studies had shown that this new reading public lapsed into illiteracy if suitable reading material was not made available which could arouse and sustain reading interests of this class of readers of all ages.

The Library's main problem was how to identify the new reading public which was spread out all over the city and organise them into groups for the serving of reading material. The neo literates graduating upto post-literacy level from the literacy centres organised by the government agencies, municipal and voluntary organisations were approached on sample basis of 10% to react to the literature available for their use.

In mid-1950 rubber soles had appeared in the Delhi market, but the conventional cobblers did not know how to fix them to the old shoes. A master cobbler was engaged and three classes were organised for the cobblers functioning around the main library in old Delhi. Similarly three meetings of railway porters were organised at the Library. Both the cobblers and the railway porters were given free shows of feature films in Hindi to attract them to the Library and they were also given light refreshment after the show.

About 10% of the cobblers and the railway porters had studied upto 5th or 6th standard. They were also asked to react to the literature available for them. In both the exercises with the neo literates and the two ad hoc groups of cobblers and railway porters, it was found that the reading material available at that time was not suitable for the reading public. Delhi Public Library was not a literacy centre though, one such centre existed in the vicinity of the Library, nor was holding of literacy classes its primary function per se. Its primary aim was to provide the available reading material to the new reading public, but little was available.

Though it was unconventional, the Library undertook the task of preparing and publishing prototype material for the new reading public. The best available authors were commissioned to write the text which was vested and edited by those who were conversant with the subject as well as the reading interests of the targeted group. In all, about 35 titles were produced in Hindi in bold type and thousands of copies were supplied on nominal price to the literacy centres and distributed to the public libraries all over the country, advising them to produce similar type of material in their local languages. The booklets were also made availabel through the fleet of bookmobiles of the Library, each carrying 4,000 books and visiting over 50 places in the city and the rural areas. Thus,the material was taken to the new reading public and delivered to them at their homes or places of work.

The project was very much appreciated all over the country and it received wide publicity through UNESCO the world over through its mass media. Since publication of literature was too unconventional a task for a library to undertake, no more titles were published, but attention of all converned was drawn to the production of such material.

MODALITIES OF ADULT EDUCATION ACTIVITIES

UNESCO in its Manifesto had defined a modern public library as follows:

"Public library is a living force for education, culture and information."

The word 'culture' should be made note of.

The Manifesto further says "A public library is taken as the practical demonstration of Democracy's faith in universal education as a continuing and lifelong process."

Never in the past, a public library had acted in India as a centre around which cultural life of the community revolved. Its services used to be confined to books only. As such, the printed word was the only medium of service. Cultural activities were never made use of to attract populance to the library. Book service is a personalised service, tailored to the needs of each individual, whereas in the organisation of cultural activities group approach was employed. The Library brought together people of similar interest. The following groups were organise from among the registered members of the library for which no fee was charged. All services of the Library were offered free of charge including the cultural activities. Each group had its own elected chairman and a secretary to conduct activities of the group. The adult education staff of the library provided only the Physical facilities and guidence. They never interfered with the autonomy of the groups. Every group met once a week in the

Library's auditorium, accomodating over two persons and fitted with coloured spotlights and microphones.

1 LITERATURE GROUP

It organised weekly open sessions where in a group member would present his or her short story or poem which was critically appreciated by the participants. Minutes were drawn by the Secretary of the Group. Book discussions were held to which the author of the book discussed was also invited to face the readers and reply to their criticism. The discussions were free and frank. the language, style of writing and characterisation were critically examined. Some of the authors went back educated and expressed their appreciation of the criticism offered by the participants. If an eminent author attended the session, the press carried the proceedings of the group. Some of the short stories and poems were published in the magazines which gave a boost to the budding authors and poets. Some of the members of the group are among the eminent writers of today and they have acknowledged their gratitude to the Delhi Public Library for shaping them up into good writers and giving them self-confidence in their writing.

2. DRAMA GROUP

The members wrote dramas themselves and if approved by the Group would be staged by its own repertory. A nominal admission fee was allowed to be charged for the plays to enable the Group to meet the expenses on hiring dresses and props for the purpose. The proceeds were handled by the Group. The playwright and the actors were not paid anything. Annual competition between the plays staged by the Group and outside repertories was held and prizes were awarded. About 4 to 6 plays were staged by the Group in a year, besides the annual competition. Some members of the Group became later became AIR artists and the dramas written by them have since been published.

3 FILM CRITICS GROUP

Documentary films were shown on predetermined themes. Not many Indian Documentaries were available in those days. Running Commentary was given in Hindi for foreign films. Prize winning films were also screened and later criticised by the members. On a few occasions actors and directors of the films concerned were also invited to listen to the criticism and reply to it. These sessions were extremely popular and the library had a few gate-crashes. No admission fee was charged for the film shown as it served as the medium for attracting the general public. At the end of the show, the viewers were approached to register themselves as members of the Library. Since library services were free, they were enrolled there and then,if they could establish their identity. A member could recommend another person for membership without any guarantee. About 10,000 members were enrolled this way within six months of the inauguration of the library on October 26, 1951 by no less a person than the then Prime Minister of India, Pandit Jawahar lal Nehru. The total membership of the Library stands today at one lakh (1,00,000) and has earned the Library the epithet of "Asia's busiest library", loaning out 10,000 books per day for home reading alone.

4 MUSIC GROUP

The members of the Group gave musical performances both vocal and instrumental music. Amateur singers over the years turned into renowned a singers and joined the ranks of AIR artists. Some of them had become so popular that the members kept imploring them to sing more and more. Some sessions lasted much beyond the scheduled timing. Soft instrumental music was relayed in the reading rooms during the lunch hour to break the monotony of reading for long hours. One day while on his routine round of the Library, the Director enquired from a reader, if he was distrubted by the soft music. he exclaimed "very much but only when it stops".

5 ART GROUP

To cater to the amateur painters, the Group organised twice or thrice a year exhibitions of paintings drawn by its members at home and those were displayed for few weeks in the Library. Mounted paintings of master Indian painters were lent out to institutions free of charge for display for a month.

6 GRAMOPHONE LENDING LIBRARY

A large of about 4,000 gramophone records and cassettes was built and lent to the members of the library of charge.

SUMMING UP

Besides book service, the projects of the library were a great success, namely publication of material for the new reading public, comprising the new literates and the school dropouts. As the Library had discovered that suitable material for the new reading public was not available in the market, it decided to publish a few titles as prototypes for the guidance of others. The effort was very much appreciated by all concerned.

The cultural activities were conducted as part of the adult education programme for the educated adults for their recreation and education as well as to draw them into the Library. The ultimate aim of the Library continued to be promotion of personal reading. Cultural activities helped in achieving the aim. About 45,000 adults participated in these activities every year. Similar activities were organised for children as well and 40,000 of them benefitted from them annually. Many public libraries in India, benefiting from the experience of Delhi Public Library are organising cultural activities to promote use of books, but none has undertaken publication of material for the new reading public as it is too unconventional a task for a library to undertake.

LOOKING AHEAD

Unfortunately, publication of material for the new reading public is not commercially viable. The Indian book market is so organised that a distributor takes a discount of 50% of the published price from the publisher and parts with 35% of it to the bookseller who sells book at published price across the counter. The average price of a book of general interest works out at least to Rupees one a page or Rs. 250/- per book of 250 pages.

The distributor makes a gross profit fo Rs.37.50 per copy sold to bookseller and the bookseller makes a gross profit of Rs. 87.50 per copy. The Library had prices its 35 titles at paise 62 per copy and if sold through the normal channel, the distributor would have made a gross profit of paise 9 per copy and the bookseller paise 22 only. It is no wonder that they refused to sell the booklets when the Library approached them and the Library had to market them itself which was for more difficult to do than publishing them.

Even of such a booklet is priced at Rs.10/- per copy, the distributor will make a gross profit of Rs. 1.50 and the booksellers Rs.3.50. It will be very small a profit to make comparted with the trade publication wherein their profit is 25 times more. Why should they deal with such material unless they are fools.

To my mind, the solution seems to lie in giving a kit of such material to the new literates before they leave the post-literacy classes on completion of the course and the school dropouts when they quit the school, at subsidised prices. In addition, free sets should be supplied to rural and urban public libraries as part of the state grant-in-aid, as selling them through market channels is not feasible. The National Book Trust should undertake publication of such material.

READING MATERIAL FOR YOUNG ADULTS

Another area which is dificient in literature is the material for the young adults in the age group of 15-18 years, dealing with career making and problems of puberty. Virtually nothing exists for this group of readers. Only a government sponsored agency like National Book Trust can undertake publication of material for the young adults as it will not again be commercially viable.

11

THE WORK OF DELHI PUBLIC LIBRARY IN THE FIELD OF ADULT AND CONTINUING EDUCATION

Dr. S.N. Khanna

1 INTRODUCTION

UNESCO, in its Paris Conference held in 1949 proposed to establish a pilot library project in one of the developing countries. Late Abdul Kalam Azad, the then Education Minister of India, was attending the said conference and he gladly accepted th UNESCO's proposal to establish a pilot library project in India. Thus, as a result of an agreement between UNESCO and Government of India Delhi Public Library came into existence.

It was established and inaugurated on 27th October, 1951 by the first Prime Minsiter of independent India Pt. Jawaharlal Nehru. A board, to be known as Delhi Library Board, was constituted to control and guide the affairs of the Library.

2 OBJECTIVE

The DPL was to carry out the policy of UNESCO Public Libraries Manifesto to provide a public library service for the people of the city of Delhi as a Model for all public Library development not only in India but also in all other countries where similar development of public libraries could be undertaken.

3 LOCATION

It was housed in a portion of a building located opposite to old Delhi Railway Station to be used as a transitory camp for the troops during world War-II. Soon its functioning grew to occupy the whole building and further spreading its wings to become a public library system.

4 A METROPOLITAN PUBLIC LIBRARY SYSTEM

The DPL is now not only a library but a well knitted public library system. Started as a small unitary library, it has since developed into a premier public library system not only in the whole of Delhi but also in the country.

The system presently includes a Central Library, Zonal Library, Branch & Sub-Branches Libraries, Community Libraries in Resettlement Colonies of rural areas, Deposit Stations and a chain of Mobile Library Service points to cover remotest urban and rural areas making the total number of service point to 173.

It has a stock of around 11 lakh books and one lakh registered borrowers taking away around 10,000 books daily for home reading, besides 3,000 readers using its Newspaper Reading Rooms every day. Around 85,000 persons participate in DPL's social edcation activities and 595 gramophone records/music cassettes are lent out daily for recreation at home. The DPL also caters to the needs of visually handicapped, patients confined to bed in hospitals and prisoners lodged in jail.

In addition to providing library services, it published a number of books and booklets for neo-literature to enrich knowledge and encourage reading habits.

5 ITS EVALUATION BY UNESCO

Since the DPL was established as a pilot library project by UNESCO, its functioning was to be assessed according to UNESCO standard. Accordingly, a survey was conducted by UNESCO and as a result of the survey, the functioning of this library was not only found satisfactory but also its work in promiting reading habits was profoundly appreciated and the DPL was declared as the BUSIEST LIBRARY OF ASIA for creating reading habits and maintaining popularity.

6 POSITION OF ADULT EDUCATION IN INDIA

Before, we go into the details of role played by the DPL in fostering adult and continuing education, let us have a view of present position. The latest Census Report of 1991 reveal a very sad picture. Out of the total population of 84, 39,00,000 there are 40,32,00,000 illiterate persons in our country. Break up among them according to per hundred is as follows as per 1981 census Report:-

Age Group	Total	Male	Female	Urban	Rural
15+	59.2	45.2	74.3	34.9	67.3
10-14	43.5	33.1	55.2	21.9	49.8
15-19	44.6	33.9	56.7	23.1	52.3
20-24	48.0	33.4	62.8	25.3	56.9
25-34	54.9	39.3	71.0	30.5	63.8
35-39	67.2	52.5	83.5	42.4	74.8
60+	78.5	65.4	92.2	59.1	83.3

The pathetic picture of our education and higher illiteracy rate is the main root of our poverty and many other burning problems. It is needless to emphasise the values and virtues of education. We know that learning is wealth to the poor, an honour to the rich, an aid to the young and a support and comfort to the aged. It is a well known fact that when we educate a man we educate only an individual, but when we educate a woman we educate the whole family.

The figures mentioned above clearly indicate that we have to launch an offensive to eradicate illiteracy by setting priorities i.e.

(i) More emphasis on rural education;
(ii) Education to weaker sections of the society and
(iii) Education to women.

7 ROLE OF PUBLIC LIBRARY

The libraries have different roles to play and according to their roles, there are different kinds of libraries such as National, Institutional, State etc. According to their functions they are further divided as Government, technical, educational, specialised libraries etc. But these all libraries are meant to serve some defined and limited set of people. A public library is a free library providing access to its resources without any discrimination of caste, creed, sex, economic status etc. Besides providing access to its resources it is to act as a community and social education centre.

8 SERVICES

The Delhi Public Library is a practical workshop to demonstrate the potentialities of a Library in fostering the reading habits and to learn as to how to behave in the society. Giving an exposure by providing a stage and forum to refine and feature of the DPL. The objective of providing reading material to all sections of the society without any distinction of caste, creed, sex, religion, nationality etc. is fully met by the DPL. The library system has a good collection of text books for secondary and higher education as well as the necessary reading material for technical, non-technical and specialised education. Besides text books, helping and research material are also made available to the students, research scholars and professionals to continue their studies. It provides reading material for formal, informal and continuing education. Book selection in the library system is made keeping in view the needs of literates and less literates adults separately. General reading material for light reading and recreation occupies a good space on the shelves. The services of the DPL have made tremendous progress in bringing library books within the reach of every citizen of Delhi and specially to those who have no access to other types of libraries. The special feature of the DPL is the nature of various library services provided by it to the adults for continuing their education through Lending, Reference and other Departments. During the year ended on March, 1991, the Library had a membership of 50,675 adults borrowing 11,97,382 books for reading at home. Besides above 2,10,449 volumes were con-

sulted by the adults in the Reference Sections of the Library system during the said period.

9 SOCIAL EDUCATION CENTRE

The DPL serves not only as a Circulation and Reference Library but also as a Social Education Centre for adults. The cultural & Social needs of the community are met by the Specifically designed activities. The Social Education Department organise discussions, debates, lectures, recitations etc. which improve reading habits and knowledge and impart training in Civic behaviour. Under these programmes interested library members are organised into groups and study circles with the assistance and guidance of the library staff. At present, the following groups are rendering valuable service and encouraging adults to imporve their talents:

(i) Literature Study Group;
(ii) Social Study Group;
(iii) Health Hygiene Group and
(iv) Home pathic Study Group.

Through discussions, debates and other activities of the library the adult folk of the society learn, exchange their views and tolerate difference of opinion. The Social Education activities of the DPL provide adults the public platform for speaking and shaping their personalities. Many members of the DPL have now occupied high positions in the society. The Library has proved bebeficial in spreading education amongst neo-literates and non-literates under these programmes. During the year ended on 31st March, 1991, 8028 adults participated in 95 Group Activities and Lectures. Besides these, 44 members were declared winners in 15 annual competitions of the Library in which 3265 adults had taken part.

10 RECREATION CENTRE

Under Social Education Programmes cultural and recreational activities for adults include film shows, television programme, drama, music concerts etc. The Drama Group and the Music Group of the Delhi Public Library have become quite popular and serve as tools to attract adults to its fold and become a member of the reading community.

The Library has no longer to propagate its recreational services for adults. In fact its recreational services are eagerly sought for. The number of recreational activities organised by the library during 1990-91 were 305 and 42,466 persons attended the same.

11 MOBILE LIBRARIES

The Extension Department of the Library through specially designed mobile vans supply books at the doorstep of the members at different points on fixed days and time. When Library on wheels was initially started by the DPL, there were apprehensions amongst the people and specially amongst the rural folk about the free library services. There were also doubts about its success. But, soon the doubts and apprehensions were removed with simplification of membership procedure on the spot and regular services of Mobile Library. Now, the mobile Library services of the Delhi Public Library have become very popular. We are having many requests for providing library services in various urban and rural areas of Delhi pending with us. The DPL has not been able to meet the demads due to inadequate infrastructural facilities. The Mobile Library had the membership of 2303 adults as on 31.03.1991 and 35137 books were issued to them during the said period. At present, the Mobile services have 66 points to serve in two shifts round the week.

As the Library cannot meet demands of all seeking library services at their localities, the DPL evolved a procedure to lend reading material to local associations or bodies to avail of library facilities called Deposit Stations.

12 SERVICE THROUGH DEPOSIT STATIONS

The DPL has provided books to public and private institutions after being statisfied that the said Institutions would provide

suitable accommodation, furniture as well as necessary staff for providing the Library services to the nearby people. This system has been functioning quite satisfactorily and generated reading habits. At present, 22 deposit stations have been serving and providing library facilities under the umbrella of the DPL.

13 SERVICE TO SPECIALISED CATEGORIES

(i) **Service to sportsmen:** The DPL has been operating three exclusive Sports Libraries at prominent stadium in the capital (a) Nehru Sports Library at National Stadium (b) Feroz Gandhi Sports Library at Talkatora Swimming Complex, and (c) Indira Gandhi Indoor Stadium Library. The accommodation for these sports libraries has been provided free in the respective stadium by the Sports Authority of India. The Library at Indira Gandhi Stadium has been started only few months back. During the year 1990-91, the first two Sports Libraries issued 9,954 books to its registered members as against 4,505 books issued during last year. More and more sports lovers are taking keen interest in reading literature on sports and are improving their knowledge and skill.

(ii) **Service to patients:** The DPL operates Library services to the indoor patients in two hospitals, viz. All India Institute of Medical Sciences and Govind Ballabh Pant Hospital. The DPL has provided books to these hospitals and these are issued to the patients by the staff of concerned hospitals. A large number of books are being read by the indoor patients of these hospitals.

(iii) **Service to prisoners:** The Library provides educational and reading facilities to the adult prisoners at the Central Jail, Tihar. It will be strange to inform that the prisoners lodged in jail themselves manage the working of the Library. This Library issued 4290 books to 567 prisoners registered as Library members during 1990-91.

14 SERVICES TO THE RURAL FOLK

The Library is fully aware to the eudcational needs of the rural areas. The DPL has two sub-branch libraries at Bawana and

Narela. In addition, Mobile Library visits 13 villages weekly and lot of library interest is being generated among the rural folk.

15 SERVICE TO VISUALLY HANDICAPPED

The Braille Library caters to the needs of visually handicapped persons. A library specially designed for the blind by the DPL was the first attempt of a Public library in India. Braille Books are not easily available and specially in Indian language i.e. Bharati (Hindi Braille). The DPL took the task of producing Braille Books and arranged to get as gift two reconditioned Braille Typewriters and some other necessary equipment as well as 500 pounds of sulphide paper. A Braille Transcribing Unit was established with the above material. The DPL had taken up with the Indian scientists and technologists to manufacture sulphide or similar paper for transcribing Braille Books. As a result, the Forest Research Institute, Dehradun perfected a process to prepare such paper. The DPL transcribes and prepares multiple copies of Braille Books for the visually handicapped persons. Besides these, Talking Books i.e. material recorded on gramophone disks or on tapes are also being served. A unit of Brailee Library has been started for University students and teachers in Delhi University campus.

The cause of continuing education is assisted by providing library service to visually handicapped persons through specially designed mobile vans issuing braille books at selected places. There are 18 such points now to serve in two shifts during a week. In addition, Braille Books are provided by the DPL at six Deposit Stations located in various institutions. Training facilities to blind people are available at the Braille Library. Braille books are also sent to the members by post, free of charge, in all parts of the country. Braille Library has been promoting the educational interests by organising annual competitions for visually handicapped, both adults and children, and winners are given prizes. The total membership of the visually handicapped adults during the year 1990-91 was 462 and 16,658 Braillee Books were issued to them during the said period.

16 FUTURE SCENERIO

No doubt, the DPL has played a very significent role in promoting literacy programmes through its multifacious dynamic planned programme of imparting informal education to the masses. But now we are heading towards Twenty First Century and the universe of knowledge has been widening very fast. The number of books and other reading material containing vast knowledge have been increasing day by day and the cost of these material has also been increasing. Public Libraries are, therefore, the best centre, which can cater to the educational needs of the whole community. In view of the growing population of Delhi, it is essential that the DPL should have more branches and sub-branches to cater the needs of newly developed areas in the urban sector as well as in the rural areas to serve as a literacy centre for weaker sections of the society and women. These expansion programmes have been included in the VIII Five Year Plan of the library. Since Delhi is a multicultured and multi-lingual city, it is proposed to establish a Bhasha Pustakalya to meet the reading requirements of various language groups. There is also a proposal to provide Talking Book Library facilities and low vision reading and reference material in Braille for imparting informal education to the visually handicapped persons. The DPL should be at the apex of all public libraries in the National Capital Region and be a coordinating agency for all development activities towards total literacy.

17 PROBLEMS & DIFFICULTIES

In India, we do not have sufficient and effective public library system. The existing States covered under library Acts do not provide adequate library services. In these Acts there is no sound provision for financial support to our libraries. The explosion in sphere of information production is getting multi dimensional exposer, whereas the financial resources already at command are shrinking.

When the Delhi Public Library was established in 1951, it was expected that all public libraries to be started in the Union Territory of Delhi will be linked with the Delhi Public Library at apex, but local authorities in the Union Territory of Delhi have started setting up libraries of their own. Now we see the libraries set up by the Delhi Administration, Municipal Corporation Delhi, New Delhi Municipal Corporation etc. There is no coordination between these libraries among themselves and the Delhi Public Library. There is urgent need for the purpose and expansion and improvement of library services that proper coordination be there amongst all library development activities in Delhi. It is also necessary that proper coordination be there with agencies engaged in promoting adult and continuing education.

For expanding the activities, the Delhi Public Library require (i) accommoadation (ii) financial resources and (iii) reading material.

Accommodation is the main constraint for exanding the activities. The Delhi Public Library can open its new branches, sub-branches and deposit stations provided it gets adequate suitable accommodation free of any charge. Community Centres and Welfare associations organised by the residents of various colonies may provide accommodation to the DPL for its expansion activities. Various institutions engaged in the field of Adult and Continuing Education can also provide suitable accommodation for opening the branches & Sub-Branches by the Delhi Public Library.

Due to financial constraints, the Delhi Public Library could not modernise and computerise its services. Information technology has been expanding so fast that it has become imperative that adequate financial resources be provided to the DPL so as to enable it to equip its services with latest information technology. For collecting reading material DPL has recently started Gift and Exchange Division. This Division acquires reading material as gift from individuals, institutions etc. and make them available to the readers. Such individuals and institutions who

are having a good collection of reading material and do not want to preserve them may donate the same to the D.P.L for the better use and preservation of the said material. This will go in a long way in building collection of reading material and to preserve them for future generations.

18 SUGGESTION

India is a multicultured society. Fostering of different cultures would keep us away from becoming unifying, intrigated and cohesive society. A chain of uniform libraries set up at local, district, state, regional and national level would not only make these libraries effective centres of dissemination of information and repository of knowledge but also ensure to be a real apostal of unifying of unifying culture and conveyer of outcome of the wisdom and intellectual activities for generations to come. To achieve this goal, the following suggestions are made:-

i) **Legislation:-** There is need for central legislation for Public Library development in the country.

ii) **Pooling of Resources:-** There should be a single authority and the resources of local, State, Central etc. be pooled on the basis of an agreed formula.

iii) **Social Education Centre:-** Public Libraries must develop auxiliary services to substantiate library activities to make it a living force.

iv) **Cooperation of local Authorities:-** The local authorities must provide functioning space for a library and its auxiliary activities to make it a real centre for cultural activities of the whole society.

v) **Public libraries in Metropolitan cities:-** On the pattern of the Delhi Public Library, public libraries be started in all metropolitan cities to meet the aim of total literacy.

vi) **Rural libraries and libraries for weaker sections of the society:-** Importance be given for expanding library activities in rural areas and amongst weaker sections of the society.

vii) **Encouragement to women:-** As the rate of illiteracy is much higher amongst women folk of the society, more emphasis be given to attract women in library activities and for their active participation.

A network of uniform public libraries fostering local culture intermingling with the state, regional and national cultures would pave a way for a unified cohensive and strong nation diminshing its divided tendencies with enlightment bestowed by these new temples of knowledge and learning. Then, there would be no obstacle to stop our march towards economic development, prosperity, everlasting peace and tranquality through the total literacy.

12

ADULT EDUCATION AND PUBLIC LIBRARIES IN BIHAR

Dr. R.S.P. Singh

India being a vast country with large population (843,930,861) has manifold problems. According to World Bank estimates India would have the largest percentage of illiterates in the world by the year 2000 A.D. i.e. it will have 54.8% of world illiterates population in the age group of 15 to 19. This indicates the magnitude of the illiteracy in the country and the urgency and importance to remove it. Simultaneously, we are facing the challange of two major tasks one of providing quality education to every one and the other of transforming the content and process of education to meet the immediate and emerging needs of the changing society. They linkage of public libraries with adult education is must for the success of the schemes.

Adult education is particularly aimed at the age group of 15-35. This scheme provides education to those, who for various reasons mainly economic or otherwise, are not able to attend regular classes of formal education. Adult education programmes, when supplimented with library services, can yield better results. A networks of libraries, covering cities, villages and adult literacy centres, can make the literacy campaign a realistic one. Some principles apply for non-formal education also.

The total area of Bihar is 1,73,877 square km. and it ranks ninth among all the states and union territories. The population of the state according to 1991 census is 69,914,734 out of which 61,195,744 reside in rural areas and 87,18,990 in urban areas. The total area of the stage constitute only 5.3 percent of the contry while the percentage of the population residing in the state is 10.51. This figure indicates that the state is densely populated with a density of 402 persons per square km. In terms of density of pupulation of the State is higher than the national density of population which is 215 persons per square Km. In Bihar 87.53 percent of the total population reside in rural areas (consisting of 67,546 villages) and 12.47 percent in urban areas.

For administrative convenience the State has been devided into 10 divisions, 42 districts, 101 subdivisions. 591 community Development Blocks and 11,968 panchayats.

In spite of the fact that Bihar has been gifted by nature with rich mineral and underground water resources, and vast cultivable areas, about 57.49% of the population is living below poverty line.

With more than 87% of its total population residing in rural areas, Bihar was not only one of the most ruralised states in the Indian union, it was one of the poorest Rural poverty, in particular, was worse in Bihar, than in any other states in India except Orissa. In this context the position of Bihar in realation to other state, is brought out by the figures in table below:-

Rural Population and the Incidence of Poverty by States 1981

States	(a) Rural population as percent total population	(b) Percent of population below poverty line 1977-78		Total
		Rural	Urban	
1. Andhra Pradesh	76.75	43.89	35.68	42.18
2. Bihar	87.54	59.91	46.07	57.49
3. Gujarat	68.92	43.20	29.02	39.04
4. Haryana	78.04	23.25	31.74	24.84
5. Karnataka	71.09	49.88	43.97	48.34
6. Kerala	81.22	46.00	51.44	46.95
7. Madhya Pradesh	79.69	59.82	48.09	57.73
8. Maharashtra	64.97	55.85	31.62	47.71

9.	Orissa	88.18	68.97	42.19	66.40
10.	Punjab	72.28	11.87	24.66	15.13
11.	Rajasthan	79.07	33.75	33.80	33.76
12.	Tamil Nadu	67.02	55.68	44.79	52.12
13.	Uttar Pradesh	81.99	50.23	49.24	50.09
14.	West Bengal	73.51	58.94	34.71	52.54
	All India	76.27	50.82	38.19	48.13

Source : (a) Census of India 1981 paper 2 of 1981
(b) Govt. of India, Planning Commission. Sixth five year plan 1980-85, Annexure 10.12 page 16.

Rural poverty in Bihar is to the extent of about 60%. This means more than half of rural population in the State is below the poverty line, i.e. having an income of less than of 3500 per annum per family. A family in the context of Bihar, would comprise on an average of five members.

The State of Bihar is quite Backward as for as literacy of the population is concerned. The sporadic efforts of the Adult Education programme (AEP) by the Govt, will not have a lasting effect unless the programmes are supported by a network of public libraries. It is recommended that the existing public libraries of various categories (State Central Library, Divisional Libraries, District Central State Libraries, Sub divisional Libraries, Block Libraries, Village Libraries) are to be enriched, developed and reorganised to take up the work of adult education by storing all kinds of books and non-book materials giving useful information about social, educational cultural and economic activities of the Govt. and other agencies. These materials should be suitably prepared with good presentation and appropriate subject matter so that they not only entertain, inform and educate the neo-literates but also would raise their mental and moral standards. The percentage of literacy according to 1991 provisional population figures is 38.54 percent as against 32.03 percent in 1981. The literacy percentage of the (38.54 percent is considerably low as compared to the all India average of 52.11 percent. Among the States other than Bihar, the literacy rate varies from 90.59 percent in Kerala to 38.81

percent in Rajasthan. Thus Bihar has the lowest literacy percentage almost at par with than of Rajasthan. In these two States, out of every 100 persons 39 are literates.

A comparative picture of sexwise literacy rates for 4 dicennial census (1961-91) are as follows:-

Year	Persons	Male	Females
1961	21.75	35.19	8.17
1971	23.35	35.78	10.24
1981	32.03	46.58	16.51
1991	38.54	52.63	23.10

Bihar lags far behind in the field of education: The matter of anxiety is that the literacy rate has been increasing very slowly as compared to other States.

Woman constitute about half of our total population. They form the vital organs of our society. They perform manyfold duties as our Mothers. Life partners as wives, sisters and daughters. In other words, in their every relation they are indispensible. If we want progress in our society, then the women folk cannot be and should not be left to continue in ignorance and illiteracy. Unless they receive education they cannot have their rightful place in the society. So education is the first thing needed here. An all out, sincere and dedicated affort should be made to make them literate so that they can join the main stream of life and can add to the advancement of national development.

Let us now have look on the literacy situation among women in Bihar. The variation of literacy since 1961 is given below:-

Year	Literacy	Male	Female
1961	18.40	29.8	6.9
1971	19.94	30.6	8.7
1981	32.03	46.58	16.51
1991	38.54	52.63	23.10

In view of the very low percentage of literacy in women, utmost importance should be given to arouse awareness in the society to teach them through all formal, non-formal and Sankul pustakalaya (S.P.) In this regard the following suggested measures may be adopted:-

1. Well palnned documentary films should be produced illustrating the advantages of being literate in running various types of house hold affairs. How a literate mother can plan better living in limited resources, (b) can save her children from avoidable ailments of both body and mind which an illiterate mother cannot do inspite of her best efforts and intention. These types of Films should have to reach even to the remotest corner of the rural areas.
2. Establishment of Mahila Mandals at village level would be very useful and fruitful. This will serve as good forums for exchange of ideas for mutal benefits. Effective implementation of social welfare measures like Family Planning etc. can be discussed there. These programmes can be arranged and sponsored by village Libraries under JSN schemes.

Growth of population and literacy among scheduled caste/ tribes in Bihar 1951-1971.

Population (lakhs) with percentage to total Literacy Rate percentage. Population in brackets.

Castes Tribes	1951	1961	1971	over	Net increase 1951-71	1961-71
S.C.	48.56 (12.1)	63.37 (14.1)	79.50 (14.1)	+30.94	6.00	6.4
S.T.	38.33 (9.5)	42.05 (9.1)	49.32 (8.8)	+10.99	9.2	11.6
Total	86.89 (21.6)	107.42 (23.2)	128.82 (22.9)	+41.93	7.3	8.4

The proportion of scheduled Castes in the total population of Bihar according to 1991 census (Provisional figure) is 14.1 and of S.T. in the total population of Bihar according to the said census is 8.8 The literacy percentage in these two sections as per 1971 Census is 6.4 percent and 11.6 percent respectively which is very low. Hence these two weeker sections of our society need special attention and care in adult education programmes.

The following table gives per capita expenditure on education 1983-84 in some ot the selected states of India. As revealed from the figures noted below among the major states of India Bihar per capita expenditure is lowest except Uttar Pradesh. This has affected adversely the quality of life of the population in the state and consequently the productivity and initiative of the man power.

S.No.	State	Per capita Expenditure on Education
1.	Kerala	120
2.	Punjab	110
3.	Maharashtra	88
4.	Tamilnadu	80
5.	Gujarat	87
6.	Haryana	87
7.	West Bengal	80
8.	Rajasthan	76
9.	Karnataka	77
10.	Bihar	54
11.	Andhra Pradesh	81
12.	Assam	79
13.	Orissa	62
14.	Madhya Pradesh	56
15.	Uttar Pradesh	49

Source: Basic statistics of Indian Economy, Vol.2. Sep 1985

THE BIHAR EDUCATION PROJECT

The Bihar Education Project (BEP) came into existence in the year 1990 with the following main goals:-

(a) Universalisation of Primary Education for all children upt 14 years of age through formal or non-formal educaton.

(b) Drastic reduction in illiteracy, particularly in the 15-35 age group, bringing the literacy level in this age group at least to 80%, ensuring that the levels of the 3-Rs are functionally relevant.

(c) Modifications in the Educational system to serve the objects of quality for women and their empowerment.

(d) Making necessary intervention to provide equal educational opportunity to adults and children belonging to the lower castes, ethnic Communities and the poorest section of the society.

The focus group in the B.E.P will principally comprise educationally and economically deprived people i.e. women and girls and the lower castes, and ethnic and tribal communities (generally referred to as scheduled caste and Scheduled Tribes)

ADULT EDUCATION

Bihar was in the forefront of the literacy campaign which was started by the provincial government in 1936-37. With the help of about 14000 volunteers drawn from students community, teachers, Inspecting Officers of Education Department, and other social workers more than 12000 literacy centres were started with an average attendance of 1.1/2 lakhs per term of six weeks. This movement also spread in Jails and almost every prisoner who was in the Jail during that period was made literate. It will be more fair to quote the name of Dr. Syed Mahmood, the then Minister of Education, Government of Bihar and Shri Gopinath Verma, the then District Inspector of schools who made significant contribution in mass literacy programme. By the year 1938 about 4000 village libraries were established in Bihar in connection with Mass literacy scheme. That tempo could not continue for a long time. Again after a long gap, the biggest thrust to adult literacy was given when the National

Adult Education Programme. (NAEP) was launched on 2nd Oct. 1978. The enthusiasm for NAEP in Bihar was clearly literacy programme. Yet the programme lost its vitality within a couple of years. The reasons for the failure of this programme was that the libraries were not attached with the Adult Education Scheme (AES) and thus the follow up programme of AES was total failure. By the year 1984-85, there were 56 Rural Functional Literary Projects and 250 State Adult Education Projects, accounting for 16,800 and 25,600 AE centres respectively.

The decline of the adult education programme visible from the early eighties became much worse during the last 5 five years. The main deficiencies of the Adult Education Programme (AEP) in Bihar are as follows:-

(1) Lack of promptness in the Government machinery, resulting in inordinate delays in the sanction of funds.

(ii) Non-payment of salary to the staff in time and non-supply of requisite teaching or learning materials. No arrangement for proper lighting of the centres.

(iii) Corruption and malpractices have gone unchecked and as such the programme could not make any impact rather it became discredited and people lost faith in the scheme.

(iv) Lack of seriousness in selection and training of resources personnel.

(v) Non involvement of dedicated and sincere people due to red tapism and corruption.

(vi) Non involvement of Public Libraries in any stage of A.E programmes.

(vii) Lack of co-ordination and supervision at all levels.

The BEP has decided to reorganise the whole programme of Adult Education through its literacy component.

According to estimates made by the Government of Bihar, there are at present about 16 million illiterate persons in the 15-35 age group. The BEP has planned to make them literate by the year 2000. For achieving this target a well defined strategies will have to be designed. But without a network of public library system it will be only a dream as happened in the past.

Another disturbing feature is that of drop-outs from schools in Bihar. Although allocation of resources on elementary education has been given higher priority over other sections of education, there is the problem of massive dropouts. The drop outs rate between class 1 to VIII is about 80% as against national rate of 70%. Again the drop outs rate between class I-V level is about 60% against just below 50% for the whole country. Of course, there are some obvious reasons for such drop-outs in a backward State like Bihar. Bihar is predominantly an agricultural State and the farmers cannot afford to lose large hours of labours by sending his child to school for a long term profitable investment. The objective of BEP is to reduce the rate of drop outs at the primary level from 60% to 45% between 1990-95 so as to check the further increase of figures of illiterates in the state.

CONCEPT OF SANKUL PUSTAKALAYA (CLUSTER LIBRARY)

In BEP document it has been mentioned that a cluster of about ten JSNs (population of about 50,000, 50 villages) will be provided with a Sankul Pustakalaya (SP) which will support structure of JSNs. A Sankul Pustakalaya (SP) will have the possibility of providing ordinary reference books, organise Cultural festivals, sports and vocational Training activities. It may take up youth development programmes, in collaboration with Nehru Yuvak Kendras (NYK), specially for women. There will be a provision for part time librarian of a SP who would be entrusted with the task of maintenance of reading room and library.. Besides it, he/she would have to act with people, with writers and artists and with researchers engaged in local language and cultural heritage. "The work of a librarian in SP will generally be assigned to a committed person who is interested in part-time work, which he/she would undertake in a spirit of social service and creativity." It is intended to set up 600 SPs by 1995. An attempt will be made to strengthen the district and state Libraries, which could provide annually a sum of Rs. 75,000/- for non-recurring cost of a SP and Rs. 25,000/- for recurring cost.

Undoubtably, the scheme of BEP and Sankul Pustakalaya (SP) is very good and encouraging but its success would depend on its sincere implementation.

PUBLIC LIBRARY SCENARIO

Realising the importance of Public Library service as a necessary concomitance of democracy and with a view to eradicate the burning problem of illiteracy, the Government of Bihar has taken steps to establish, develop and strengthen public libraries at different levels. Such libraries established so far in Divisions, Districts, Sub-divisions, blocks and villages provide opportunities to the reading community for life long self education and carrying the torch of knowledge and learning. Thus public libraries in this state are scattered right from state capital to villages. A brief description about those libraries is given here.

STATE CENTRAL LIBRARY:- The Smt. Radhika Sinha Institute and Sachchidananda Sinha Library was converted to the status of the State Central Library by a deed of Agreement between the Trustees of the Library and the Government of Bihar on the 24th November 1955. It posseses a grand repository of valuable cultural treasures and has made highly significant contributions to the cause of education in this historic state by catering to the needs of teachers, students, scholars and enlightened members children, women and neo-literates of the community. It is significant to mention that the Library is utilised with considerable profit by research scholars of different Universities of India and abroad. Besides its varied collection of upto date books on different subjects, the Library has a rich store of journals, periodicals, newspapers old and current which are not available in any other Library in the region and which are of considerable importance for studies and research. In the words of Pandit Jawaharlal Nehru:- "This library is undoubtedly something of which Patna should proud". Mr. Horace I. Poliman, Chief India Section, Library of Congress, Washington, D.C. had visited this Library on 13th March 1947 and mentioned: "This Library is one of the finest public libraries in India. It was particularly interested in the excellence of Indian collections. There are many books on India which the Library of Congress would be proud to own, and which are owned by this Library. The citizens of Patna can be proud of this distinguished collections.

Now the total collection of this library has reached 1 lakh 50 thousand with staff strength of 37 in all.

The library has various sections- (a) Reading room, (b) Lending Section, (c) Local literature section, (d) Children and Neo-literates Section, (e) Braille section (f) Research Sections etc. to cater to the needs of the reading public. A magnificent building is under construction to enlarge various activities.

***DIVISIONAL LIBRARIES*:-** Since there are 10 divisions in the state, there will be public libraries located at each divisional headquarters except Patna division where state central library is already there is existance. At present there are only seven divisional libraries. The old district central libraries located at seven district headquarters, (which have become the divisional headquarters due to creation of new divisions) have now been converted into divisional libraries.

***DISTRICT LIBRARIES*:-** In the year 1953-54 of First Five years plan libraries were established in all the 17 districts headquarters of the state with an intention to setup a complete network of library organisation from the State Central Library down to the village libraries and the establish a system of class co-ordination and co-operation between the libraries at different levels.

Now there are 42 districts in the State out of which ten district headquarters have been converted into divisional headquarters. Consequently there will be 32 district libraries against which we have 25 district libraries uptil now. Thus remaining seven newly created district headquarters have not been provided with district libraries.

In district libraries group-there are two types of administrative set up, (a) Government district libraries (b) Aided district libraries.

Out of 25 district Libraries, 5 district libraries called 'District State Libraries' were established by the Government and are pure government libraries. The remaining 20 district libraries called as 'District Central Libraries are govt. aided libraries. These library get annual grants for Establishment, purchase of books and Journal and contigencies. The Govt. has created seven posts for each District State library while four for each district Central Library.

***SUB-DIVISIONAL LIBRARIES*:-** The total number of Sub-Divisions in the state 101, in which 42 are sadar sub-divisions and 59 are Mofassil sub-divisions. At present 20(twenty) sub-divisional libraries exist in Muffasil Sub-divisions. Thus out of 59 Muffasil sub-divisions 29 sub-divisional libraries are yet to be established because 42 (forty two) Sadar Sub-divisions will have no sub-divisional libraries because Divisional and District Libraries already exist there.

There 20 S.D. Libraries get annual grants from the State Government for establishment, purchase of books and journal and contingencies. The Government has also created two (a) Librarian (b) Sorter, for each Sub-Divisional Libraries.

***BLOCK LIBRARIES*:-** Out of 591 blocks in the State so far 440 block libraries have been set up as block libraries so far. Besides the supply of selected purchased books, the government and RRRLF scheme a sum of Rs. 300 per block library per year was to be given. But this is not regular. These libraries exist mostly in rural and sub-urban areas, but their collection and maintenance is very poor.

***VILLAGE LIBRARIES*:-** As per the Directory of the public libraries in Bihar published in the year 1966 a total number of 4422 village libraries existed in the state. But according to a later report now the number of such libraries is 4000 only.

These libraries get grants mainly in form of books selected and purchased by the Government under the Scheme of central purchase and Raja Rommohun Roy Library Foundation. The Government used to sanction and grants for construction and repairs of building & furniture also. But this is not regular. The present condition of the majority of village libraries is deplorable. They need special care and attention.

LIBRARIANSHIP TRAINING COURSE:- At present the Education Department is spending 9000/- per annum on librarianship training course. The post-graduate certificate course is of 3 months duration and held once in year in Sinha Library Campus in order to meet the demand for more sub-professional and junior personnel for different types of libraries. The seat is limited to 70 only per year.

So far 1550 graduate trainees have received the certificate of post-graduate training of library course from the state government of Bihar. The undergraduate course is of one month and held once in a year of four divisional headquarters, at Patna, Muzaffarpur, Bhagalpur and Ranchi. The seat is limited to 50 only per centre per year. So far 3220 students approx have received their training in one month librarianship course. Successful students of the certificate course in Library Science have opportunity of their employment in school and colleges, Public Libraries, Government Departmental libraries and public sectors in sub-personnel and junior positions.

LIBRARY LEGISLATION IN BIHAR:- The Government of Bihar directed the librarian of the Sinha Library Dr. R.S.P. Singh in the year 1973 to submit a draft of public library bill to State government. The draft was considered by a duly constituted sub-committee consisting of some eminent librarians of the State. But the State Government's effort in this direction is not much encouraging and the matter is still pending. There leaders of the State like Dr. Jagannath Mishra, Shri Guneshwar Pd Singh & Prof. Nagendra Jha took interest in this matter but frequent changes of the Government. But still the people in library professions have no lost their patiance.

***FINANCING OF LIBRARY SERVICE*:-** Public Library Service in the State is mainly financed by the State Govt. The State government provides the total annual funds for a sum of Rs. 37 lakhs from Non Plan & head which is very meagre to meet the expenditures on various heads-like establishment, contingencies, purchase of books and magazines & furniture, building construction & repairs etc.

In the changed circumstances when utmost importance is being attached to the non-formal education, mass literacy campaign and adult education, the existing libraries should be strengthened and re-oriented to meet the requrements of the public. For this the provisions for adequate allocation in the states annual budget and allotment of funds in time would be necessary.

CONCLUSION

The alarming figure of illiteracy in Bihar (61.46%), lower standard of education, economic and industrial backwardness are subsequently due to deplorable status of public libraries. The so called (4501) public library, are not truly according to standards laid down by UNESCO. They are not rate supported, nor administered by legislation, but are run on subscription and inadequate government aid, as such their services are no satisfactory. They suffer from paucity of funds, upto-date collection, modern furniture and fixture, functional building and professionally qualited staff. Low status of librarians and conservative and unqualified people in top line management is also responsible for poor condition of libraries. Nothing has been done seriously so far to establish the network of public libraries. If Bihar has to be dragged out from acute stagnation and curse of poverty the development of infrastructure including a network of public library service is sin-qua-non without any further loss of time. The library service should provide full facilities for literacy campaign and continuing life long education. This pious objective can be achieved only after establishing a network of public libraries based on Library legislation which is pending for final decision with the State government since 1973. Considering the situation of adult education and public library in Bihar the following measures are suggested for improvement and achievement of desired goals:-

1. All categories of public libraries now rendering service to the public as an independent and isolated units should be united into one single system of State Library System.
2. Adequate annual funds be provided to the Public libraries for the purpose of fostering and promoting the spread of knowledge and removal of illiteracy.
3. A separate Deptt. of Public Library be created headed by a professionally qualified person with adequate experience in the field of State Public Library Service.
4. A separate wing for Adult Education be established in Library Directorate for co-ordinating and monitoring the work with the deptt. of Adult Education & B.E.P.
5. The public libraries should be reoriented to take up the work of adult education by stocking all kinds of books & non-book materials for neo literates & work actively in follow up programmes of A.E.
6. A separate Book Development Council should be established by the state govt. for neo literates. The govt. should encourage local authors, publishers and illusrators who may produce standard, useful and attractive materials suited to the needs.
7. A State Advisory Committee be constituted to coordinate the Adult Education programmes with the Public Libraries and other voluntary organisation and institutions.
8. A detail register of Public libraries & voluntary organisations be prepared at the State level after spot survey who may contribute in AEP & B.E.P.
9. Efforts be made to select, collect and display the educative films among the illiterates and neo-literates with the help of Library & Adult Education staff.

10. Workshops and seminars be organised at regular intervals for exchange of ideas in order to improve the quality of work.
11. More than 4500 existing Public Libraries of various categories which are functioning as independent isolated units should be integrated into one chain of State Library System for the total benefit of the community.
12. The annual allocation of libraries be fixed between 6 to 10 percent of the State Education budget as per guide lines given by the "National Policy on Library and Information system".
13. The book collection should be updated and a special section for illiterates and neo-literates be started soon in all public libraries.
14. Audio-visual facilities be provided to attract illiterates and neo-literates.
15. The working hours of the library be fixed to serve the people more effectively.
16. Mobile library unit should be attached in urban and rural areas as well.

13

JANA SHIKSHAN NILAYAMS—UNDER PUBLIC LIBRARY SYSTEM

A CASE STUDY OF ANDHRA PRADESH.

Dr. V. Venkatappaiah

During the Pre-independence days, the adult education centres, then called as night schools were maintained as one of the activities of the public libraries. In some cases primary schools also conducted this programme. After independence and particularly after library legislation the librarians, as professionals felt that organising of adult education centres was not their responsiblity. At the same time, authorities have not bothered any thing on this important issue. Consequently, both these areas were separated by administrative operation of the twins. Even at the time of National Adult Education Programme (1978), National Literacy Mission (1989), and even in the present Total Literacy Campaign (1991) the place of libraries in adult education programme was completely ignored, resulted a very poor performance of post literacy programme and continuing education for neo-literates and the second part which is now remained on paper only.

In this connection, it may be noted here, that the 44th All India Adult Education Conference held at Calcutta during October, 1991 felt that "post literacy programme of adult education was not started at Kerala so far", when Kerala was declared as totally literate in April, 1991 through *Akshara Keralam*. If it is the case what will happen to the neo-literates? By this time they might have lapsed into illiteracy. If it not true.

I will be happy, if some body from Kerala reacts on my statement. In the light of the issues, we will now examine relationship of public libraries and adult education at conceptual level.

PUBLIC LIBRARIES AND ADULT EDUCATION

The integral connection between Public Libraries and Adult Education was recognised at international level as early as 1949 when delegates from 29 countries met at Denmark at the International Conference on Adult Education passed the following resolution, "The Conference records its recognition of the essential contribution of Museums and Public Libraries to Adult Education. Appropriately to the circumstances of each Member-State, the Conference supports UNESCO's Proclamation that the Public Library-a living force for popular education, culture and information and recommends its consideration and so far as possible, its adoption in Member-States, as a basis of policy".

DR. RANGANATHAN'S PLEA

Dr. S.R Ranganathan, the formerly National Professor of Library Science in India stated that old victorian inventory outlook revelled in meticulous care and accuracy in maintenance of stock of books is not order of the day and formulated the Laws of Library Science viz., Books are for use. He stressed that adult education programme should be integral part of the public library service, in his book "Education for Leisure".

SHRI IYYANKI'S VISION :-

Shri Iyyanki Venkataramanayya, the Father of Library Movement in India stated, that it is high time for us to understand and recognise that the library has a key role both in the creation and fostering of the yearing in the adult for his own uplift through self education and literacy. "To us Library is a social service centre, for the whole village, where human activity trabbed with life and animation for up lift of the country. What a temple has been till about a hundred years ago, our library strove to be, and was during the first half of this century, and a couple of decades proceedings to it" says Andhra Ratna. To this end, the library should function once again as social centre and foundation source of human once again as social centre and foundation source of human activity in every village and urban area. During the days of freedom struggle, hundreds of village libraries in Andhra area took special interest in adult education and literacy including education for women.

ADVISORY COMMITTEE'S SUGGESTION

The Advisory Committee for Libraries headed by Shri K. P. Sinha, formerly Director of Public Instruction, Government of Bihar, in his report (1958) emphasized that libraries are primary institutions for educational advancement of the people. As such, they are one of the agancies of social education and stand in close relationship to other similar agancies. The relation of libraries with educational or potentially educational groups, for that is what brings it in the orbit of social education. The Committee stressed that liquidation of literacy is the concerned not merely of the individual, but also the community as a whole. It should be treated as permanent importance of the day.

REVIEW COMMITTEE'S RECOMMEDATION

The review Committe appointed by Government of Andhra Pradesh (1976) headed by Shri Gopala Rao Ekbote, retired Chief Justice of Andhra Pradesh stated that the most effective role that libraries can play in adult education is that of helping the people to help themselves. Libraries should strive to be less dominated by a "Print mentality" and place more reliance on the use of non-book materials. It is this material, which is going to help the libraries in organising a campaign of removal of illiteracy from the rural areas. Public Library services obviously have an important role in supporting follow up literacy compaign in fact public library movement can not be separated from the anti-illiteracy movement, since neo-literates need books and other reading materials to enable them to conserve and expand knowledge which has been obtained by them. It recommends the Government to constitute an agency on a permanent basis or entrust this to Public Libraries after strengthening the department to fight against illiteracy on a war footing, so that the agency could carry on the work mostly in rural areas.

STATUTORY OBLIGATION

Section 13 (I) (F) of the Andhra Pradesh Public Libraries Act, 1960 states that the Zilla Granthalaya Samsthas (Dist Library Authorities) have the obligation to provide the lectures, and the holding, of classes and conduct of other activities connected with public library service including social education. Following the provisions of the Act, the Zilla Granthalaya Samsthas are conducting cultural activities, wherever possible, in stray cases running an adult education centres. However, it should be accepted, that the public libraries, in recent years have not bestowed much attention on Adult Education, for various reasons.

S L C RESOLUTION

In the light of the National Adult Education Programme, the State Library Committee, an appex body to advise the Government of Andhra Pradesh on the development of Public libraries, in a recent, meeting decided that the libraries should co-operate in conduction Adult Education programme, and where ever possible, the librarians may conduct literacy classes during their working hours, without detriment to the normal functioning of the library. They can even conduct the Adult Education classes, even after closing the library and on holidays. Most of the libraries have the opportunity of functional buildings, qualified staff well equipped furniture, well selected follows up literature and a congenial atmosphere. These assets can be put to proper utilisation.

We will now examine the role of these twins (i.e.) public libraries and Adult Education in the dessemination of knowledge in the pre independence days.

ADULT EDUCATION CENTRES IN ANDHRA PRADESH

Andhra Pradesh had its roots of Adult Education in the second half of 19th century. It appears that Andhra Evelongilical Luthern Church, Guntur started the Adult Education Centres, as a part of their programme to spread christianity in the masses. So also, Brahmo Samaj, a new social and religious organization opened prayer Samajam to popularize the movement in the beginnings of this century though the languages of the country. A disciple of Brahmo Samaj, Shri Kandukuri Veeresalingam attracted the people through his simple style and developed a craze in learning a language. Besides this, Lord Curzon's division of Bengal, and the Swadeshi Movement drove the budding youth to think about their own country and politics became a subject of discussion to the youth. The people, who realised the importance of the situation started instutions like National Schools, Public Libraries, Rural Schools and the Adult Education Centres. At the first instance, Night School were started at Rajahmundry by the leading students of Govt. College Education, Rajahmundry. This was followed up by starting Adult Education Centres as night schools located in school buildings and public libraries. Shri Sanivrapu Subbarao, who is supposed to be the Father of Adult Education movement in Andhra Pradesh started the Refresher Courses in the name of Rural Reconstruction Programme in 1929. Influenced and inspired by this programme Prof NG Ranga, Ex MP resigned his job at Madras Presidency College and joined in the freedom struggle. In fact Prof NG Ranga started the Adult Education Centre in Nidubrole in 1933, which was inauguarated by Mahatma Gandhi. Such Adult Education Centres were organised in many places Circar and Rayalaseema Regions. Taking this opportunity, Shri Sanivarapu Subbarao organised Andhra State Adult Education Conference at Chagallu in West Godavari in 1937 and formed Andhra State Adult Education Association for follow-up action on the resolution after the conference. The British Government observed that all these activities were conducted against the interests of the Government. The Govt felt that these centres are developed as places of "think tanks" for freedom fighters. To curb these night school activities, the British Government banned the organisation of Adult Education Centres in the State. As per this order, one has to obtain the permission of the Police Commissioner of the State or the District Collector to organise or open an Adult Education Centre. This order badly effected the functions of existing Adult Education Centres. To meet the situation, a State level Adult Education Conference was organised at Tanali in 1941. After the conference was over Shri Gadicherla Harisarvottamarao led a delegation to the British Government. Ultimately the British Government could withdraw their ban orders. This situation helped to start many Adult Education Centres by the voluntary organizations in the State in the year 1942. Adult Education Movement saw its heights in that year. But, it is unfortunate that most of the volunteers of Adult Education went to jail in the freedom struggle and the movement gradually sink down for want of leadership and proper guidance. The same is the fate for library movement also.

SECOND PHASE 1947-1978

During the second phase many organisations, Education Department, Panchayat Raj Department of the State Governments encouraged the starting of Adult Education Centres. A Literacy House was opened in the premises of Andhra Mahila Sabha, Hyderabad in 1971 with the financial assistance of Government of India. Andhra University started the Adult Education Department. Even though Adult Education Centres were functioning in many places in the state, there was systematic organization to control or guide them or moniter the activities. Besides this, there was no production of post literacy sufficiently for sustaining the literacy among neo-literates. Due to these reasons the progress of Adult Education Centres it is nominal only after independence.

THIRD PHASE 1978-1991

By 1978, Government of India entered in the scene in a big way and launched National Adult Education Programme in all the State and Union Terriotories, with a clear motive that "literacy should be regarded as way of preparing man for a social, civic and economic role that goes far beyond contours of rudimentary literacy training consisting of merely teaching of reading and writing". Under this programme, 52 Adult Education projects are started in the State to make literate 11 million adults of age group 15-35. Besides this a number of voluntary organizations involved in this programme. In a period of ten years the Andhra Pradesh State could achieve ten lakh adults literate. But unfortunately, the ranking of literacy in Andhra Pradesh State as per 1981 census was in 23rd palce, but in 1991 census it was stepped down to 25th place, which is below the national average. Realising the pitfall, the Government of Andhra Pradesh with the support of Government of India, Total Literacy Campaign (T L C) was launched in all districts in the State. Each district is spending to a tune of Rs. 3 to 6 crores for this programme.

DRAWBACKS OF THE PROGRAMME

The main drawback of the campaign is that it lacks a well planned structure of Jana Shikshan Nilayams (JSN). It may be possible to organize literacy programmes with the volunteers. But the JSN must necessarily be centre-oriented. Conceptually, JSN includes programmes of a Charcha Mandal, Youth Club, Mahila Mandal, Library and reading room. In fact, all these activities are being organized by the library movement of the pre-independence days and to some extent even in the existing public library system under the APPL Act, 1960. What, I would like to impress on you is, that literacy part of the Adult Education programme can be retained with the Adult Education Department, which had necessary infrastructure to maintain it. The second and third areas of work (i.e.) post literacy work and continuing education can safely be entrusted to the Department of Public Libraries of the State, where the Library Act is in operation. So far 10 States have library legislation. The States and Union Territories are in various stages passing library legislation. However, the Government should insist on the States to pass library legislation and entrust work of JSN's to the Dept. of Public Libraries and provide necessary funds to operate the programme effectively. The reasons for entrusting the work of JSN's to the Department of Public entrusting the work of JSN's to the Department of Public Libraries are mentioned below.

1. The objectives of the JSN's and a Public libraries are more or less the same.
2. The public libraries under a public library system had the benefit of well trained staff to maintain the libraries or JSN's on regular basis.
3. Basically, the public library equip with reading material for the neo-literates and in the phase of continuing education.
4. The public libraries are generally located in good buildings, equipped with furniture, fitting and located in a congenial atmosphere.
5. Above all public libraries, if maintained on a statutory basis must have audit, inspection and accountability with a systematic monitering, control, direction and supervision of the Government.

TOTAL LITERACY CAMPAIGN-A SUGGESTION

It appears, that the Govt of India, with a partial support of the States, introduced Total Literacy Campaign (TLC) in 70 districts in the country before the end of 1991. The official sources revealed, that during the Eight Five year plan TLC's will be introduced in 350 district more, out of a total 457 districts in the country. The plan is extremely good, and if it implimented properly in out country will be fully literate by the end of Eighth Five year plan.

I have the opportunity to see some of the PLAN OF ACTION REPORTS of the districts, where TLC is in operation. I find, that the JSN's part is very feable in these reports. Very recently, when the district administration entered in the field, a misconception was developed that *adult education* means *adult literacy* only, and in some cases writing signature is literacy. This is the area where a check is needed from the Govt. of India.

While approving the scheme of TLC in the district, the Govt of India, should examine the capacity of the district adminstration or the District Literacy Mission to provide a network of a JSN's in the entire district in sufficient member as a continuous programme as specified in the guidelines. In this connection, it is to be noted that JSN's, should be centre based, which is an effective mean for learners to interact among themselves and with the Statics and then help the process of learning. These should not be any time lag, between literacy and district literacy phase and it is better to start JSN's even before starting the Adult Education Centre's, to create an atmosphere. Any way, my suggestion is no to approve any TLC, when it is not fully supported by a network of JSN's and their continuity, to fulfil the objectives of National Literacy Mission, effectively.

14

ROLE OF PUBLIC LIBRARIES IN ADULT EDUCATION IN ANDHRA PRADESH

Dr. GVSL Narasimha Raju

Public library movement in Andhra Pradesh is a people movement. Voluntary organisations were enthusiastic and acitve involving themselves in literacy, library and was contributing a great deal towards adult education programmes. Few individuals also did pioneering work. Libraries and adult education programmes were going hand in hand. With the passing of the Andhra Pradesh Public Libraries Act, 1960 and with the public libraries coming under its purview the situation changed. The law is silent on adult education by public libraries. Adult education should form part of library services in a State. Where there is library law adult education should be entrusted to the Directorate of Public Libraries.

Early Public Libraries and reading rooms can be traced in Andhra Pradesh even during the 19th Century. One such reading room established in 1839 at Rajahmundry, a moffusil town in Andhra by an English gentleman, James Thomas, who was the then District Judge was very popular. People were waiting for the reading room to open at six O'clock in the morning. The reading room provided a Telugu News paper *Vrittantini,* some English books and many Telugu books.

But it was from 1910 onwards Public Library movement in Andhra inspired the people of the region and set example for other states. The movement was inspired by the nationalist movedments of early 20th Century and emulated the spirit of the Library Movement in Baroda State promoted and patronosied by Maharaja Sayojirao II. Drawing a distinction between the two Library movements Dr.Ranganathan observed "whereas the Library Movement in Baroda was patronised by the Gaekwad himself the Library Movement in Andhra Desa was entirely a people' Movement". The main architect of this popular movement was Shri Iyyanki Venkataramanayya.

These early libraries were taking up adult literacy programmes by organising night schools for adults as their adjuncts. They were also participating in many social activities like organising popular lectures; celebrating local and national festivals and national events like birth and death anniversaries of national leaders of prominence. Some Libraries organised debating competitions and games and some were even active in occasional *'Annadana'* (free meal distribution) programmes. Home delivery of books to ladies free of any charge was common. It was also a common practice of most of the libraries to read alcud news papers and magazines, useful books, and classical literature like 'Puranas' for the benefit of the illiterate. Some libraries were even publishing pamphlets and booklets for the benefit of the neoliterates.

Shri Iyyanki Venkataramanayya says that "if some of the adults did not go to the library to hear the librarian reading out from books, papers and periodicals, the librarians himself used to go to places where they generally congregated for gossip, namely in the vicinity of the tank bund. The bunyan tree, the temple pial or the like. He used to take part in gossip, and make his presence and knowledge felt among them, in such a way that in course of time they could not do without him and were impelled by an irresistible inner urge to go to the library and then gradually to the night school.

Keeping in tune with his zeal for propagation of literacy, libraries and knowledge Iyyanki vehemently pleaded saying that "the duty of a librarian, especially in a village, is not only to lend books to those who can read but also to attract the illiterates to the library and to give them orally information and knowledge contained in the papers, books and periodicals on every problem confronted by the illiterate persons in their daily life and routine and thus strengthen, by judicious advice, the urge for literacy gradually created in them. The librarian should get acquinted with every illiterate in his village or area of service, understand his problems, sympathise with him and attract him to the library ultimately to make him capable of using books in which he would find his true and never-failing friends and guides".

The Andhra Desa Library Association, which is later renamed and at present known as Andhra Pradesh Library Associtíon did great service to the cause of adult education. Early in 1920 the Association organised an adult education school for 20 people and again in 1934 for 32 people. During 1941 to 1955 the association conducted Training Courses for librarians and volunteers. In these courses library movement, spreading of adult education and national movement, spreading of adult education and national movements were publicised with considerable detail. Besides these training courses training camps of lesser duration of 3 to 5 days were organised for library workers and knowledge about adult education was imparted.

Even in 1920's the Association was passing resolutions at its annual conferences urging the public to seriously think about ways and means of educating the adults. When the Government of Madras passed an ordinance on 11th June 1941 prohibiting adult education movement on the plea that this movement was responsible for spreading communism in Andhra the Andhra Desa Library Association opposed the move by convening a Special meeting at Tenali in Guntur District. The meeting passed resolutions condemning the move and resolved further to 1. publish pamphlets and books for adults 2. organise adult education classes for one hour every day 3. select teachers who can go round villages and spread knowledge 4. use magic lantern to develop scientific attitude in the people. As a result of the Association's statewide reaction on the ban of adult education programmes by libraries and voluntary organisations the Madras Government ultimately withdrew the ban orders. Even today the Andhra Pradesh Library Associtíon publishes articles and poems and brings out special issues on adult education, in its official organ.

GRANTHALAYA SARVASVAMU

Shri Gadicherla Hari Sarvottama Rao, President of the Andhra Desa (now Andhra Pradesh) Library Association for 25 years since 1938 did pioneering work in adult education. Even as a student of LT class Rao started a night school in 1907 thus sowing the seeds of adult education in Andhra. In 1937 when Indian National Congress came to power in the various states people were hoping that literacy movement would be given a boost. In Madras State even though the Government was silent in the issue Shri Hari Sarvottama Rao and others were still enthusiastic about adult education. Adopting new methods they prepared readers which will help the illiterates to become literate easily trained several students, young people and teachers to participate in the adult education campaign. He also prepared books which were useful for the adult education instructors.

Immediately after Independence in 1947 the Government at Hyderabad and Madras both were taking interest in adult education programmes. They established training centres for adult education instructors and trained hundreds of primary school teachers. These centres were given liberal grants for teaching aids and for libraries attached to them. Books and periodicals were supplied to the reading rooms of these training centres. Shri Hari Sarvottama Rao was appointed Honorary Director for Adult Education in Andhra region. He did great service for the cause of adult education by travelling extensively in the region and inspiring people to take up adult education as a natinal cause. He was also associated with south India Adult Education Association and was the Chief Editor of its jornal the *Adult Education Review* for a long time.

In Andhra Pradesh, besides the Christian Missionaries some of the political organisations, voluntary organisations, youth organisations and student organisations actively participated in the literacy movement. Individuals like Goparaju Ramachandra Rao, Yellamanchili Venkata Krishna Rao wrote books which were very popular and were used for adult education. Even ladies were very active. Every 'Mahila Mandali' (Women's organisation) in different towns in the State was taking up literacy programmes. Some of these organisations are still active, Andhra Mahila Sabha under the leadership of late Smt. Durgabhai Deshmukh established at Hyderabad 'Saaksharata Bhavan' (Literacy mansion) which is still every active. State Adult Education Resource Centre, Adult Education Instructors Training Centre, Adult Education (Social Education) study Centre and population study centre are functioning from here. For her pioneering work Smt. Durgabhai Desmukh was awarded Nehru Literacy Award in 1971.

In almost all aspect of adult education and literacy movement the public libraries used to play a prominent role as has been described earlier. However, with the implementation of library legislation in the state the one time popular intermix of public library services and adult education has lost its tempo. There is no provision to read classics, or books or new papers to the illiterate in the public libraries of the ZGS. Only posters are displayed. These public libraries do not undertake to run night schools or take up training adult education instructors. The link is almost lost. A few voluntary organisations which have libraries/reading rooms still conduct adult education programmes. But as private libraries they may or not be receiving any grant-in-aid from the Zilla Granthalaya Samsthas. The Andhra Pradesh Public Libraries Act, 1960 was silent on the matter of public libraries vis-a-vis adult education.

The Government of Andhra Pradesh appointed two different committees—one under the chairmanship of Shri Gopalarao Ekbote to review the provisions of A.P.P.L. Act and the functioning of the public libraries in the State and another under the Chairmanship of Shri Vavilala Gopalakrishnayya to review the functioning of the Aided Libraries. The first Committee's report was submitted in 1977 and the second committee's report was submitted in 1977. Both committees were aware of the need for adult education programmes and literature for neo-literates. The Ekbote committee suggested that "The State Central Library should be responsible for the production of literature for neo-literates and children of different age groups and blind people". Vavilala Committe suggested that each of the grant-in-aid Private libraries may be given a grant of Rs. 1,000 per annum for stocking reading material useful for neo-literates and taking up adult education programmes. However, not much progress can be seen in the area of modern public libraries in the State getting' involved in adult education programmes.

The author in his Doctoral Dissertation on the *Effect of library legislation on public library development in Andhra Pradesh* (1982) emphasized the need for interlinking adult education with public library service. He suggested :

1. The Directorate of Public Libraries be entrusted with adult and social education activities. This should be included in the duties and functions of the Director of Public Libraries.
2. The Director of Public Libraries should be assisted by three Deputy Directors-one for administration, one for technical service like centralized processing, compilation of bibliographies, union lists etc., and the third Deputy Director 'to look after taining requirements of personnel and adult and social education needs to shape libraries as community cultural centrs'.

It is further suggested by him that at the District level the present secretary of the Zilla Granthalaya Samstha may be redesignated as District Library Officer and may be charged with adult and social education programmes in addition to library services and effective implementation of the provisions of the Delivery of Books Act. It is suggested again that for these functions the District Library Officer should be assited by three Deputies.

SUMMARY

Literacy and library movements were closely related in the early 20th century in Andhra Pradesh. Pioneers in Public library movement were doing great service for the cause of adult education. With the passing of the A.P. Public libraries Act the old glory of enthusiastic people participation in adult education movement was missing. The link between libraries and adult education can no longer be seen except in the case of very few institutions run by voluntary organisations. Efforts should be made to link adult education with libraries. The A.P. Public Libraries Act shoud be suitably amended and adult education should be entrusted to the Directorate of Public Libraries with similar provisions at District level.

15

LIBRARY PROFESSIONAL ASSOCIATIONS AND ADULT EDUCATION

Prof. Krishan Kumar

The importance of literacy is universally recognized. Literacy can bring qualitative change in the life and environment of the people. But the task of providing literacy is a country like India is a daunting one. On March 1, 1991.[1] India's population stood on 843.93 million. The literacy rate being 52.11 per cent. Thus, there are ove 404.16 million illiterates.

The National Literacy Mission (NLM) was launched on 5th May, 1988. The primary aim being to start a mass movement, to mobilize volunteers for literacy work to impart literacy to 110 million illiterates in the age group of 15-35 years by June, 1995 [2]. Jana Shikshan Nilayam (JSM) is a concept in continuing education under the NLM. IN Feb, 1988; Government of India decided to establish JSNs all over the country in a phased manner. The aim being to institutionalize post-literacy and continuing education so that those who have achieved literacy do not lapse into illiteracy. JSN includes "programmes which were being organized as part of farmer's training programmes, rural radio forum and *Charcha mandals*, young clubs, mahila mandals, mobile and village library system, rural reading rooms etc."[3] It is established for a cluster of villages. It performs a variety of functions and serves as a library, a reading room, an information window for providing information on various developmental programmes. Thus, a rural public library forms an integral part of a JSN.

SIGNIFICANCE OF LITERACY

A literacy programme aims to convert illiterates into literates. This would result an increase in the number of potential users of libraries, leading to greater use of libraries shows that progress in literacy gives boost to the development of libraries especially public libraries. Therefore, one can say that librarians have vested interest in the increase of literacy.

STAGES OF LITERACY

We may recognize the following stages of literacy:

(a) Pre-literacy stage,
(b) Literacy stage and
(c) Post-literacy stage

Library associations have a role at all the stages. They can be involved at the planning stage, in the creation of awareness among illiterates, in the identification and inspiration of people to come forward to become volunteers. They can even take up the job of turning illiterates into literates.

NATIONAL POLICY ON LIBRARY AND INFORMATION SYSTEM

National policy on library and information system document[4] was issued in 1986. The document gives great importance to literacy and describes the role of libraries in the promotion of literacy. The national policy has not been passed by the Parliament as yet. Library associations especially the Indian Library Association should work towards the acceptance and implementation of the same.

PARTICIPATION AND INVOLVEMENT IN LITERACY PROGRAMMES

Due to significance of literacy programmes, library services to *preraks*, decision makers, literacy agencies, those undergoing literacy, neo-literatés, etc should get high priority. This should be the urgent and most significant message of the associations to their members. Library associations can propagate among its member librarians the need for greater identification and involvement of librarians in literacy programmes. library associations should work out strategies to achieve greater involvement of librarians.

The message should go to librarians that they must adopt most modern techniques of marketing to reach the target population. They should make efforts to create awareness about literacy among illiterates by means of extension services. Adequate reading materials, effective and efficient services should be provided to those undergoing literacy and neo-literates. It is a special responsibility of libraries especially public libraries that neo-literates are not allowed to lapse into illiteracy.

LIBRARY STANDARDS

Jana Shikshan Nilayam (JSN) is a concept n continuing education under National Literacy Mission. A JSN is established for a cluster of villages. If performs a variety of functions and serves as a library, a reading room, an information window for providing information on various developmental programmes. Thus, a rural public library forms an integral part of a JSN.

Indian Library Association (ILA) should set up standards relating to organing a rural public library, which is an integral part of a JSN. This may cover standards for equipment and furniture, building, qualifications of the staff, collection, services, etc. It should also undertake the responsibility of establishing a few model public libraries.

ILA should impress upon the central and state governments to establish JSNs not only in rural areas but also in urban areas as well. These could be located in public libraries, wherever feasible.

PUBLIC LIBRARY

A public library should become an information centre. Traditional library services should be combined with other information services based on oral tradition and media other than printed word. Its services should be integrated with literacy compaigns.

A large public library should have a separate adult education section. An adult education section is responsible for extension services. ILA should set up standards relating to organization of an adult education section of a public library. The standards should also take care of extension services.

SCHOOL LIBRARY

ILA should set up standards relating to an extended school library serving the needs of the public including neo-literates. The standards for an adult education section and extended school library would have certain common features.

The standards relating to a JSN, a public library and an extended school library may cover the following aspects:

1. Collection
2. Services including extension services: This should cover reading lists and different levels, serving different regions
3. Furniture, equipment and bulding,
4. Qualifications and qualities of staff
5. Mobile van library, boat library, bullock cart library.
6. Network of Public libraries

For the network of public libraries. A network would assure access to reading materials and audio-visual aids to neo-literates so that they do not lapse into illiteracy. A well developed network would be able to play its role effectively in promoting literacy programmes at various stages (pre-literacy, literacy and post-literacy).

Library association, at State and national levels, have an important role to play in the enactment of public library legislation. Indian experience shows that professional organisations have been quite active in this regard. A library legislation enables a State to establish and maintain a network of public libraries, which is essential for the promotion of literacy.

COMPILATION OF READING LISTS INCLUDING AUDIO VISUAL MATERIALS

The reading list should include books, periodicals, audio-visual materials, etc. These may be prepared for different regions.

These may compiled under the following three categories:

Materials for pre-literacy (illiterates) stage to create awareness (motivation) to become literates. These may consist of posters, films, audio-cassettes, video-cassettes.

Materials for literacy stage (neo-literates). The aim being to serve the needs of neoliterates. This kind of literature can be graded into grade 1, grade 2 and grade 3.

PUBLICATION PROGRAMME

The compilation of reading lists would indicate the gaps. Knowing the gaps, the library association can then approach the publishers and authors. Librarians need to work together with authors, illustrators and publishers to produce literature for neo-literates and those undergoing literacy, to serve the needs at different levels. The librarians should also repackage information for them in a user friendly form appropriate to them. This could take the form of a poster or a booklet or some audio-visual form.

HOLDING OF SEMINARS/CONFERENCES

ILA should organize seminars/conferences at the national level to propagate greater identification and involvement of librarians in literacy programmes. These can also be used for formulation of standards and strategies for reaching illiterates, those undergoing literacy and neo-literates. State library associations can also hold seminars/conferences at the State level to fullfil the above purposes.

TRAINING

In a village, a *prerak* or a school teacher can conduct literacy classes and also look after the library. *Preraks* and school teachers need to be trained in establishing and running a library and a reading room attached to a literacy centre. This could be an integral part of JSN. The training should be imparted by librarians. A library association (at national and state levels) can organize such a training programme. A manual can be developed for providing guidelines for organizing a library.

Separate training programmes can be established for librarians working in library or in an extended school library. Specific programmes would be required for different levels of staff.

LIBRARY AND INFORMATION SCIENCE EDUCATION

Libraries have an important role in the promotion of literacy. Therefore, topics such as -literacy and library associations; literacy and academic libraries; literacy and public libraries; basic knowledge about illiteracy-should form an important component of the paper on 'Library and Society' at B.Lib.Sc. Level. Students at MLISc level, can be asked to write project reports on these topics. At MLISc level, a separate paper on 'public library system' can also cover different aspects of 'literacy and libraries' as discussed in this paper. ILA should approach library schools and convince them for the inclusion of the above mentioned topics in the curriculum.

NEED TO ESTABLISH LINKAGES BETWEEN LIBRARIES & LITERACY ORGANIZATIONS

The public libraries should have linkages with organizations/individuals running literacy programmes. They should reach out to illiterates, those undergoing literacy programmes and neo-literates. For this purpose, extension services should be strengthend. Library associations can motivate librarians to give high priority to the provision of extension services.

The linkages between public libraries and literacy agencies are extremely weak. The fault lies with both. Somehow, library associations and librarians especially public librarians have been by and large ignored by those responsible for literacy programmes. They have not been associated at any stage of these programmes. For the long range success of a literacy programme, it is desirable that librarians especially public librarians must be fully involved at each stage, right from planning to implementation covering pre-literacy, literacy and post-literacy stages. It must also be admitted that librarians have not taken sufficient interest in this area. The situation can be rectified, if professional organizations make an effort to motivate librarians to participate effectively in literacy programmes. During 1920 to 1948, social workers were trained by Andhra Desa Library Association, who conducted night classes in villages. Somehow, this stopped after the enactment of Public Libraries Act, 1948. This is a good example of linkage between a library association and literacy programme.

As President of ILA, the author had taken an initiative and submitted a proposal in 1989 to national authorities to hold a National Seminar on Role of Libraries in the Promotion of Literacy Programmes. However, there was no positive response. The fault lies with both. Librarians have not associated experts in literacy programmes in planning library services for neo-literatures. The bridges have to be built up.

From above, it should be clear that there is a need to establish linkages between library associations (including librarians) and agencies running literacy programmes. Both have a common objective that of creating a reading public.

KNOWLEDGE

In order to carry out reading promotion activities successfully, a librarians (used in the broad sense) should have basic knowledge and understanding of illiteracy. This is equally true, whether he is a professional, a semi-professional or non-professional. In courses on library and information science, he must be imparted this kind of knowledge.

RESEARCH

We do not have a clear idea about what role the libraries can play in literacy and post-literacy processes. We know very little about how neo-literates seek information. We need to find out the ways to reach them effectively. Another matter of concern is how librarians can work with different agencies engaged in literacy programmes? Therefore, there is a need to carry out research into these aspects. The library associations should encourage research into this area.

EDUCATING DECISION MAKERS

There is a need to change the attitude of government and those of various individuals and agencies involved in literacy, towards libraries. The decision makers concerned with adult education need to be educated that libraries have an important role to play at different stages especially at the post-literacy stage. They need to be told emphatically that unless free acess to libraries is made available to neo-literates at post-literacy stage, then they are bound to lapse into illiteracy. Library associations should make all efforts to convince the decision makers in this regard.

STRENGTHENING OF LIBRARY ASSOCIATIONS

From above, it becomes clear that library associations have an important role to play in the scheme of thing. However, we need strong associations, so as to be able to play their part effectively. Had they been strong enough then they would have taken the initiative and done intensive lobying to achieve the rightful place for librarians in literacy programmes. The need of the hour is to carry out lobbying with state and national agencies to redefine the place of libraries in literacy programmes.

As it is, by and large our library associations (national and state ones) are weak. Some are berely alive. We should aim to strengthen them, by increasing the number of members and also go for broad based participation of members. They should build up their resources through provision of consultancy services and publication programme.

My humble plea is to strengthen library associations, both at the National and State levels, so that they become truely representative of the profession and are in a position to play their role expected from them.

ISSUES FOR DISCUSSION

- (i) Changing the attitude of the Government, decision makers and other involved in literacy compaigns, towards libraries.
- (ii) Instituting and implementing of national policy on library and information system.
- (iii) Creating appropriate linkages between the library professional and literacy agencies.
- (iv) Redefining of the role of libraries especially public libraries in the promotion of literacy, in the context of the changing environment (library is being now considered as an information centre).
- (vi) Establishment of a network of public libraries and strengthening of school libraries.
- (vii) Provision of adequate extension services.
- (viii) Formulation of standards for establishment and maintenance of libraries.
- (ix) Training of librarians.

CONCLUSION

Public libraries are best suited for post-literacy and continuing education programmes. However, public libraries in India are week and a neglected lot. A strong network of public libraries would prove to be an asset for literacy programmes. School libraries can also play an important role in a literacy programme. By and large, school libraries are in a bad shape. It is desirable that school and public libraries are strengthened so that they can play their role expected to them.

At present only ten States have enacted public library legislation. It is desirable to have library legislation in each state and also take steps to strengthen school libraries so that these can serve as extended school libraries.

In view of the importance of literacy for the progress of a nation, public and school libraries should give high priority to literacy programmes. They should have strong linkages with organizations and individuals running literacy programmes and reach out to illiterates, those undergoing literacy programmes and reach out to illiterates, those undergoing literacy literacy programmes and neo-literates. Library associations can propagate among its member librarians the need for greater identification and involvement of librariens in literacy programmes. Decision makers and librarians, school librarians and library associations at each stage of literacy right from planning to implementation. Thus, linkages between those concerned with literacy and library profession can be strengthened for success of literacy programmes, vital for the progress of the nation.

REFERENCES

1. *Indian Express* (Delhi edition), March 26, 1991, p. 1 and 9.
2. *National Literacy Mission,* New Delhi, Deptt. of Education, Ministry of Human Resource Development, Govt. of India, 1988, p. 14.
3. *Jana Shikshan Nilayam,* New Delhi, Deptt. of Education, Ministry of Human Resource Development, 1988, p. 3.
4. *National Policy on Library and Information System-a Presentation,* New Delhi, Ministry of Human Resource Development, Govt. of India, 1986.

16

TRAINING LIBRARIANS IN ADULT EDUCATION CONCEPTS AND CURRICULUM

Dr. P.S.G. Kumar

The role of a modern public library is just what a temple had been till about a hundred years ago. In those days temple used to be the nerve-centre of various social, cultural and spiritual activities of a village. Under the present changed circumstances, the public library shall have to play a similar role. It has to enter into the very heart of the life of village. The view that the library is intended only for those who can read and write is obsolete and partially correct. The public library should take special interest in adult education and the activities alike.

ROLE OF A LIBRARIAN

A glance at the working of public libraries in India since the beginning of the present century till we attained in dependence show how our people had struggled hard to run them and to make them devote themselves to the cause of learning and for the fuller development of the individual. In fact, no activity which contributed to the reconstruction of the society was considered beyond the scope of the library's work.

MODUS OPERANDI

Attracting People: The library worker used to go to places where the adults generally congregate for gossip, namely in the vicinity of the tank bound, the village banyan tree, the temple pial or the like. By taking part in their discussion, he used to make his presence and knowledge felt in such a way that in course of time, they could not do without him and were impelled to go to the library.

At the Library: After attracting the people to the library, the librarian used to read out to them daily passeges from news papers, periodicals and books on their choiest topic at certain hours convenient to the illiterates. Thus the habit of going to the library and interest in literacy were created in them.

The Night School: The third stage was running the adult literacy classes. Many of the adults in villages had their own occupations to pursue during the day. Time and methods (which were some times add) had to be moulded to suit their convenience. The interests of illiterate adults among the masses are diverse and spread over such a vast cross-section of the society that no uniform preparation on the part of the librarian or adult education worker will always be of assistance to him in performing his duties. The village librarian gathered a group of enthusiastic literates and with their help and cooperation maintained a night school and imparted adult education and literacy.

IYYANKI'S MESSAGE

The librarian just like the Pandit of the temple should sit on the pial of the library and go on reading some attractive and useful information from books and periodicals and consequently the very existence of the library in a licality first catches the people's eye **(Druvshyam)**, then the ear **(Sravanam)** and ultimately the mind **(Aydhyanam)** and thus our mission of eradication of illiteracy and adult education will be achieved to the maximum extent and context.

TRAINING OF THE LIBRARY WORKERS

The village library workers should be trained in adult education and other literacy programmes so that they could equip themselves fully for the successful execution of the task. The duty of a librarian, especially in a village is not only to lend books to those who can read but also to attract the illiterates to the library and to understand the information requirements of the adult illiterate and provide the needed information. These activities will make the illiterate realise the need to learn to read and write. Thus they will be initiated into the adult education programme.

EFFORT MADE EARLIER

Having felt the need for training librarians in adult education work, the Andhra Desa Library Association conducted several training classes from 1920 onwards. Several books on adult literacy including teachers guides and books for literacy classes were also published by the Association. Some efforts were also made by the Madras University and Baroda State in this direction in 1920s and 1930s.

LITERATURE

A detailed course curriculum and guide for teachers was prepared by Shri G Harisarvothama Rao (Past-President of Andhra Desa Library Association) in Telugu. This was very Popular. Shri K.G.G. Sundaram also wrote a guide book for teachers in Telugu on 'Adult education'. A 'Handbook for Teachers of Adult Illiterates' was prepared by the Central Adult Education Committee of the National Christian Council, Nagpur. A 'Handbook for Social Education Material Writers' was published by Literacy House, Allahabad. Similar works were published in Hindi also. Important among them are

by Uttam Singh Tomar;
by Mahesh Dutt Pathak; and
by Acharya Badrinath Verma.

TRAINING PROGRAMME

Need

Various governmental and Voluntary organisations have been carrying out the adult education programmes since long. We have seen how library workers were playing an important role in adult education and in non-formal, perpetual and self education.

It is a matter of regret that the Government as well as other agencies concerned with adult education have ignored the role the libraries can play in adult education and self education. The village library workers have also lost their ethusiasm. It is therefore, necessary to chalk-out a training programme for library workers in adult education perpetual self-education to villagers and educationally disadvantaged.

Courses

State level library associations should organise special training programmes for rural library workers and those interested in adult-literacy programmes centred round libraries and who are prepared to serve as 'Adult Education Workers' in collaboration with librarians.

Secondly, the University departments should offer 'adult education' and 'adult library work' as an optional paper at BLISc level.

Content

I am giving here under a syllabus that can be considered as a basis for courses outlined above.

Importance of Adult Education: Learning is fundamental. Learning through reading and writing. Learning and writing in ancient period. Literacy as key to development and success of democracy. Non-formal education and adult education. Role of school teachers, librarians and social workers in adult education. Need for training adult education workers. Campaign for eradication illiteracy. Programmes with special reference to India and the concerned state.

2. **Aims:** For better living conditions: To overcome exploitation; To read and write letters; To know as to how to make applications and submit memoranda to government; to know the new techniques in production, new products, etc. To behave as a better citizen-By knowing the voting right and right exercise of the power; For better enjoyment of life through reading

newspapers, story books, etc. Service to neo-literates and providing life-long education.

3. **Psychology of Adults:** Difference between a child and an adult with regard to their knowledge, experience, grasping power, impact of reading, thinking capacity, reflection of the society on the individual, etc. Inhabition and shyness to learn at an advanced age. Planning adult education programmes in the light of his work, surroundings and living conditions-vocabulary, examples, illustrations, elaborating the subject, etc.

4. **Programme Planning:** Starting with a prayer, songs and music, lessons punctuated by short stories; Inspiring talks, discussions, etc; Revision of old lessons or previous lesson; new lesson; roll call (attendance); discussion on day-to-day problems of the village and villagers, contemporary social and political situation; and ending with a prayer or song.

5. **Qualities Needed in an Adult Education Worker:** Softness, free from egoism, easy mixing-up with people, no status-consciousness, understanding, knowledge, knack of presentation, eloquency, patience, sympathy towards mistakes committed by the trainees, encouraging, no eye on remuneration or returns, etc.

6. **Teaching Techniques:** Select compound and complex alphabets which are very common; select simple and homely words; use story method; suppliment with illustrations; increase vocabulary in a progressive manner; use standard alphabet charts; use latest techniques of teaching alphabets; Give special stress on use of related alphabets and contexts of use; Give special instruction with regard to pronounciation.

7. **Teaching Aids:** Black board and chalk; Lamps; Alphabetical charts; Atlases and globes; readers; Charts; slides; specimens; tapes; films; projection equipments; Public address system; Education Games; aids for teaching mathematics; etc.

8. **Publicity:** Importance of libraries through lectures, exhibitions, radio talks, television programmes; Role of libraries in adult education and non-formal education; library extension activities; book mobiles, inter library loan services; library

services, sections of a library, local collections; writing; newspaper articles; special publicity materail and their distribution in local fairs, festivals, etc; Special meetings, lecture programmes, etc.

9. **Projects and Programmes:** National Regional and local

REFERENCES

1. HARI SARVOTHAMA RAO (Gadicharia) Vayojana Vidya bodhana kramam (= Course for adult education). Ed 5 Vijayawada: AP Library Association, 1967
2. Kumar (PSG). Role of Libraries in adult education. In ROUT (RK), ED. Library legislation in India. New Delhi: Reliance, 1986.
3. NAGABHUSHANAM (Paturi). Vayojana Vidya Granthalaya (Adult education-Libraries). In Granthalayamulu Part 1. Pedapalem: Sewasram, 1972.
4. VENKATARAMANA YYA (Iyyanki). Light of the library. Vijayawada: World Federation of Wisdom, 1973.

17

TESTING OF PROTOTYPE BROAD-SHEETS FOR NEO-LITERATES IN WEST BENGAL AND TAMIL NADU

Tilak Mukherji and Dr Deepa Das

BACKGROUND

The overall efforts of the National Literacy Mission, and specifically in the Total Literacy Campaign (TLC) districts, have coverted about 20 million illiterates to neo-literates. It is known that unless these neo-literates practice the newly acquired skill they tend to lapse into illiteracy. The present environment and effort is not too conducive in encouraging this practice. As a result there is a real danger of large scale lapsing leading to severe frustration and wastage of national efforts and resources. We can draw an analogy from "it is better to remain blind, than to again sight and lapse into blindness".

In this context, NIAE has proposed a device to encourage the practice of the literacy skills among the neo-literates-a weekly broadsheet in several languages, for the TLC districts. This can serve the purpose of providing enjoyable and appropriate reading material, widely, regularly and on a continuing basis.

NIAE has carried out formative research to help design the broadsheet. A viability study has also been conducted to assess the issue of basic relevance among the target group, publishing and distribution mechanism (via the newspaper system), and nature of the content.

Based on the formative research, NIAE has developed two prototypes-Jog a jog in Bengali and Thenril in Tamil. These are in a ready to use stage.

These prototypes were field tested with two very specific objectives, discussed below:

Delivery: Village to neo-literate

The viability study addresses the issue of reaching the broadsheet up to the village level through the existing newspaper channel. The next step, village to neo-literate, still remains. This study seeks to assess the situation after the broadsheet has been reached to the village level. Basically, it attempts to estimate exposure, reach and readership among the end target group, once the reach to the village is ensured. In other words, the focus here is the grass root level dissemination.

Reader Response

The second objective is to ratify the prototype which was developed based on formative research, and provide inputs to improve it. The parameters are overall appeal, comprehension, vocabulary, and content.

DESIGN & METHODOLOGY

Grass root level dissemination

This was an operations research study. Copies of the broadsheet were reached to the village level by NIAE through the District Administration. The facilitator who received the copies in a village then ensured reach to the neo-literates. Interviewers visited such villages 3 or 4 days after the copies had reached and conducted the study as follows:

- In-depth interviews with the facilitator (sarpanch, volunteer, opinion leader etc)
- Observation of spots where copies might have been displayed for the public

Random survey of neo-literates (based on available lists at the centre/village) to determine exposure, reach readership, source of knowledge, place of reading etc

The plan and coverage is indicated below:

	Bardhaman	Medinipur	PTT
No. of Villages	10	10	28
No. of Facilitator	20	18	17
No. of neo-literates	248	219	236

The fieldwork was carried out during May-August 1992.

READER'S RESPONSE

This was obtained after engineering full exposure to the broad-sheet. Interviewers placed a copy with frandomly selected neo-literates (from village/centre level list), allowed over an hour of reading time, and then interviewed the respondents. A semi-structured questionnaire was used.

The plan and coverage was:

	Bardhaman	Medinipur	PTT
No. of Villages	10	10	20
No. of neo-literates	152	148	144

DISSEMINATION: VILLAGE TO NEO-LITERATE

Delivery system up to the village

For this operation research, we depended on the District Administration. The two states seemed to have followed somewhat different channels. In West Bengal, the route was Collector's Office to BDO to Gram Panchayat to Village facilitator or Volunteer.

The Tamil Nadu system differed a little. The TLC project infrastructure was more involved. The route was Collector to District Programme Officer or Asst. Project Coordinator to the next level to the Panchayat to the village organiser/volunteer.

A general constraint voiced in all the district relates to the number of copies made available. Whereas 5 copies per centre was planned, in reality fewer copies actually reached each centre. This must be borne in mind while assessing the reach and impact. Perhaps the time gap between delivery and study was too short. A longer duration might have yielded better results.

It is amply evident that the extent of reach within a village depended to a very large degree on the initiative of the village facilitator and volunteer. Hence, engineering dissemination within a village is not a difficult task. For example, in Medinipur, the proposed visit by the Block President motivated the volunteer to ensure wider coverage. As a result, the performance is distinctly better compared to Bardhaman. And, the PTT experience has its own story to tell.

Reach and impact

The table below gives an overview of the exposure and reach, among All, Males, Females:

	Bardhaman			**Medinipur**			**PTT**		
	All	M	F	All	M	F	All	M	F
Did not see	75	72	77	48	59	33	19	35	14
Seen but not read	9	7	11	15	11	21	13	10	14
Read	16	21	12	37	30	46	68	55	72
Base (Neo literates)	248	109	139	219	125	94	236	60	176

It is heartening to note that despite paucity of copies and time, te actual readership level can be as high as 72% (Female, PTT). Even the figure of 37% (All, Medinipur) fares very well vis-a-vis the readership levels enjoyed by large dailies. Our point is that if this is a planned and concerted effort, with the help of the volunteers, a fair level of readership can be reasonably expected.

The other promising cue is that there are *very few who saw the broadsheet but did not read it.* This supports the premise that the broadsheet fulfills a felt need gap of the neo-literates, and that if exposure is ensured then readership will follow.

Those who read the broadsheet spent on an average of about: Bardhaman-50 minutes-75 minutes, PTT-60 minutes. This is true for both men and women and goes to show the efforts made by the neo-literates in practicing their new skills. Also, the number of copies is to be determined such that the neo-literates can all read an issue over a week's time.

The volunteer and the literacy centre emerges as the main catalyst, as was stated earlier. This is evident from the fact that in a majority of the cases the source of knowledge and exposure is the volunteer/centre:

	Bardhaman	Medinipur	PTT
Where seen?			
Literacy centre	84	73	75
Source of knowledge			
Volunteer	76	81	95
Base (Those seen)	62	114	190

It must be added here that our observation found virtually no instance of display of the broadsheet in a public place.

The conclude, given the scenario obtaining today, if the broadsheet is reached to the village, there is bright prospects in terms of reach and readership. In this context, it is worth noting that the success hinges critically on the volunteer. The plan needs to recognise this and make adequate provision for volunteer motivation and cooperation.

RESPONSE TO THE BROADSHEET

The contents of Jog a jog and Thenril were different, and to that extent not amenable to generalised conclusions. The indicator of success is the degree of retention of the items, as reflected by top of mind recall (or saliency), which is a function of interest, case of reading and appeal. Saliency of an item could be governed by one or more of these factors: Subject, Space occupied, Position in the Broadsheet, and Visual support.

For Jog a jog, the more salient and least salient items are indicated in the table below. The response is near identical between men and women, hence All figures and shown

% recalling spontaneously

	Bardhaman	**Medinipur**
Pisciculture	73	84
Ayodhya	63	78
Bank loan small	45	69
Scheme for small farmers	39	66
Story-Sawa kilo chaal	28	64
Literacy before marriage	46	68
Hooghly-100% literate	30	57
Vidyasagar	25	41
Trees & environment	61	36
-		
-		
Hike in textile prices	10	5
Women's bank	13	4
Semia	18	4
Hike in rail fare	16	5
Base (Neo-literates)	152	148

A further analysis of the more salient items shows this:

Item	**Subject**	**Position**	**Visual**	**Space**
Pisciculture	Economic	Front, top	Yes	Medium
Ayodhya	Politics	Front, top	Yes	Large
Bank loan-housing	Economic	Front	No	Small
Scheme-small farmer	Economic	Front	No	Small
Story-sawa kilo	Story	Front	No	Large
Trees & environment	Environment	Back, Top	Yes, strong	Large

The least salient items all appear on the reverse. Two are small and without visuals (textile & rail). The Semia story is large, on the reverse and with visual. Perhaps the subject is not too attractive. It has been voiced that the interview method of the Women's bank feature is perhaps alien to neo-literates, and hence less relatable. Such approaches perhaps is best introduced gradually.

While not concluding about the contributing factors, it is prudent to consider these aspects for deciding upon the content of the broadsheet.

The Thenril spontaneous recall scores are:

% recalling spontaneously	PTT
LTTE & Rajiv Gandhi	52
Women police	51
Cattle feed	47
MGR film song	45
Puzzle	39
Short story	38
Sarla Devi (social worker)	36
Letter from editor	31
Home remedies	29
-	
-	
Olympics	15
Letter from neo-literate (running Hand)	11
Hike in rive price	17
Word game	16
Base (Neo-literates)	144

An analysis of these items show:

Item	Subject	Position	Visual	Space
LTTE	Politics, Violence	Front, top	Yes, strong	Large
Women police	Women, Law & order	Back, top	Yes	Medium
Cattle feed	Economic	Back, top	Yes	Large
MGR song	Entertainment	Back	Yes	Large
Puzzle	Entertainment	Back	Yes	Small
Short story	Story	Back	Yes	Large
Sarla Devi	Social work	Front	Yes	Large
Letter from editor	-	Front, top	No	Medium
Home remedies	Health care	Back	Yes	Large

Olympics and the letter from a neo-literate are both on the front and fairly prominent. Rice price is also on the front but occupying lesser space. The word game is at the back and prominent. Perhaps the subject in some cases, reading and comprehension difficulty in other cases (letter in running hand and word game) could be the reasons for low appeal and recall.

The net learning in sofar as content design is concerned is that we need to actively consider the aspects of subject, position, visual support and space.

The fact that the overall level of response is high in all districts, is heartening. Our contention is that the researches have indicated the broad framework. An optimal design can emerge only after a few trial runs and with regular feedback from the readers.

Moreover, change and improvement is likely to be inherent and continuing as a process for the editorial content.

The overall reception to the broadsheet has been positive. Both men and women have spontaneously responded with enthusiasm. This ratifies the basic concept of the broadsheet.

The level of positive response nearly touches the 100% mark across all districts. The reasons stated relate to Information, Environment, News, Entertainment etc. The figures for negative response or lack of response are: Bardhaman-3%, Medinipur-0%, PTT-0%. In research terms this is indeed a very positive feedback.

Upon specific probing, negatives or areas of dislikes do not emerge at all in West Bengal. However in PTT, nearly 60% have some comment to make e.g.:

	PTT	(%)
Disliked	***Male***	***Female***
Puzzles, story	0	21
Olympics	0	12
Film song	20	11
LTTE	16	12
Base (Neo-literates)	49	95

The intensity of negatives is low, However, it is worth taking into account the little hints, from both men and women, to fine tune the content.

One anxiety was the literacy competence of the neo-literates in reading the broadsheet:

(%)

Read the broadsheet	Bardhaman	Medinipur	PTT
With lot of difficulty	1	4	6
Little difficulty	52	44	13
Easily	47	52	82

An observation is that in all districts, more, men responded 'Read easily' than women. It is worthwhile paying greater attention to the aspect of vocabulary and sentence construction.

An issue was the type size used:

(%)

Type size	Bardhaman	Medinipur	PTT
With lot of difficulty	1	4	6
Need large size	6	9	68
Size alright	91	87	5
Need smaller	3	4	27
Base (Neo-literates)	152	148	144

The response pattern is similar between men and women. From this, it seems that a larger size for Thenril could be considered.

In terms of suggestions for improvement made by the neo-literates, the prominent and actionable ones are:

- Greater visual support
- More news on agricultural advances (method, techniques, implements)
- More sensational news (PTT)
- Bigger type size for puzzles (PTT)

In sum, the prototypes created pass the acid test. Cues for improvement has been obtained, and to the extent feasible, should be incorporated. It seems that certain types of articles are difficult to absorb at this stage (interview, word game) May be, these can be introduced gradually. The overall design based on the formative research stands ratified, in terms of vocabulary, type size, content etc. The broadsheet is also enthusiastically received.

THE FINAL ANALYSIS

The broadsheet as a product is vindicated in all respects. The improvements, as emerging from the study, if carried out will only make these stonger.

The dissemination from the village to the reader is also viable given the current system. With planned effort, a fair degree of reach and readership is reasonable to expect. The volunteer is a key person, and the centre the catalyst. We must consciously evolve plans keeping these facts in mind.

The issue of publishing and distribution up to the village level has been addressed separately.

18

THE VIABILITY OF A BROADSHEET FOR NEO-LITERATES

Tilak Mukherji and Dr Deepa Das

BACKGROUND

The National Literary Mission has made intensive efforts towards bringing up the level of literacy. These efforts were even more intensive in Total Literacy Compaign (TLC) districts where over 20 million illiterates have been converted to neo-literates since 1990.

It is important that the neo-literates practice the acquired skill to reach the end objective of greater self reliance. Otherwise, it is proven, lapsing occurs i.e. the newly converted neo-literate tends to revert to the status quo ante, that of illiteracy.

The natural environment is not conducive for the practice and application of these skills. At present the efforts in this direction are inadequate. Therefore, the post literacy focus and task is the retention of the acquired skill among the neo-literates, so that the mission objective is met in letter and in spirit. The end objective is to ensure that the neo-literate is indeed empowered and achieves self reliance, and that the mammoth effort and investment is not wasted. Else, there will be severe frustration at both the beneficiary and the programme levels.

To encourage the practice of the newly acquired skill among neo-literates, the need is to provide enjoyable and appropriate reading materials with wide and regular distribution, on a continuing basis. The vital conditions for this to succeed are that it should be effective, efficient, sustainable and replicable on a nation wide basis.

Given these criteria and objectives, the prima facie choice was a weekly broadsheet for neo-literates along the lines of a newspaper in terms of publishing and distribution. Obviously, this will have to adhere to certain technical guidelines in terms of vocabulary, type size, and sentence construction.

Having evolved this conceptual model, NIAE conducted a research study to assess the viability of such a broadsheet, prior to progressing the idea further.

THE STUDY ISSUES

The study addressed the following broad issues:

- The feasibility of the newspaper route in terms of publishing, and distribution upto the village level
- Feasibility of the concept as a means of inducing and ensuring the practice of the acquired skill of the neo-literates
- Design of the broadsheet in terms of the nature of its content
- Feasibility of an alternative channel of distribution through the distributors of consumer products of large companies,in rural areas

DESIGN & METHODOLOGY

A field study was conducted in five TLC districts viz. Chittoor (Andhra Pradesh), Panipat (Haryana), Kamarajar (Tamil Nadu), Durg (Madhya Pradesh), and Bardhaman (West Bengal).

The target group comprised:

Experts-Functionaries, officials, volunteers associated with TLC, local opinion leaders, etc.

Newspapers-Editors/proprietors of district/block level newspapers, Officials of mainline/metro newspapers

Beneficiaries-Neo-literates, men & women, who have completed Primer II and are in the 16-45 years age group

Distributors-Of major companies marketing consumer products in rural arears

A multi-method approach was necessary. Both quantitative (using a structured questionaire), and qualitative (using an in-depth guide) personal interviewing techniques were used.

A pilot study was carried out in Durg prior to launching the full fledged all India study. The pilot exercise helped in fine tuning and finalising the design, instruments, and methodology.

The questioning followed the funnel approach, from the very broad to the specifics. The dialogue began with the people, changes in society etc., moving onto the literacy campaign and its impact, motivations to join, need for information and access to media, response to the idea of a broadsheet for neo-literates, and finally specific reactions to the concept in terms of content, pricing, distribution etc.

The coverage/sample size was:

	Chit	Kam	Pan	Brdh	Durg
Newspapers	14	6	6	19	9
Exports	17	18	23	16	25
Beneficiaries (in-depth)*	82	76	79	82	72
Beneficiaries * (structured)	200	200	200	200	200

* Equally split between men and women

The field survey was conducted during Feb-March 1992.

This paper takes up and discusses the issues in the following sequence, concluding with directions from the study:

- The contextual framework, comprising the literacy campaign, the beneficiaries, and the infrastructure available for publishing
- Assessment of the publishing and distribution scenario
- Inputes for the design and content of the broadsheet
- Overall promise of a broadsheet among the beneficiaries, indulding the pricing factor
- Directions from the research

THE CONTEXTUAL FRAMEWORK

The literacy campaign and the people

The overall response of the various segments interviewed is positive and optimistic. The experts, functionaries, volunteers, and opinion leaders feel that the total literacy campaign is now emerging as a movement in the districts.

This movement has cut across age, sex, caste, religion, and is truly a universal phenomenon. In fact, this has also had significant impact in heightening the importance and increasing the pull for primary education. An actual quotation of a volunteer illustrates the intensity:

"TLC is running so well that if an instructor does not take one class, the higher ups are informed immediately by the learners"

At this juncture it is important to understand the neo-literates slightly better. This will provide the back drop while the issue of distribution and design/content is addressed.

Some key indicators are shown below:

% of neo-literates

	Chit	Kam	Pan	Brdh	Durg
Pucca housing	27	13	23	1	1
Electricity	55	32	16	1	42
Radio	51	26	59	43	47
Television	5	2	37	1	1
Wrist watch	31	37	62	39	44
2 wheeler	3	1	23	0	15
Men					
Married	70	28	73	50	95
16-24 years	25	78	44	65	39
Women					
Married	91	37	61	60	78
16-24 years	50	79	45	69	44

Considering all indicators, it seems that the socio-economic status of the neo-literates is the highest in Panipat and lowest in bardhaman. The marital status and age profile are not uniform across the districts, which has a direct bearing on the design of the broadsheet, particulary in terms of interest areas and types of information.

The specific profile of each area must necessarily be borne in mind while designing the broadsheet. The above provides a broad idea of the characteristics of each district.

The next parameter is the reach of various media among the neo-literates. This indicates the importance of information and the desire to know among the neo-literates, and provides the basic rationale for the proposed broadsheet.

% of neo-literates at all listen/see/visit

	Chit	Kam	Pan	Brdh	Durg
Radio	91	74	67	90	82
Television	51	52	72	55	68
Cinema	97	83	17	61	31

Reach of radio among the various entertainment media is the highest, which is not surprising given the fairly high ownership of radio sets. However, despite the virtual absence of television in the neo-literate household, its reach is not insignificant. Cinema continues to a be popular source of entertainment in the East and South.

In view of this media scenario, there is ample evidence to support the thesis that the neo-literates not only have a need for entertainment, but also a desire to know about the world around them. This again supports the rationale for a broadsheet.

The final evidence to justify the post literacy effort in preventing lapsing is adequately indicated by the sentiments articulated by the neo-literates. It is in this context that the broadsheet needs to be assessed in terms of its viability. Some actual quotations best portray the picture:

"Used to see educated people reading and writing. I also wanted to be like them..."

"Others in my village were attending the centre. I thought why should I lag behind. When women and children go, why cannot I"

"When government has started something it must be useful"

"To be able to count my wages"

"My son used to read and write letters for me. I did not like it and used to feel bad. So I joined"

"I did not know what my children are doing in school"

The net emotion is perhaps most appropriately summed up by the words of a female neo-literate in Kamarajar:

"Before joining the centre we were like the blind, although having eyes which can see. To make myself self-dependent I joined the centre"

It is established beyond any doubt that the literacy campaign has touched the right chord of the illiterate masses. Just as there was a strong need to become literate, there is an equally strong desire to stay so in order to reap the end benefits of the new content with merely being made neo-literates. They wish to remain empowered and attain self reliance and control over their immediate environment.

And therein lies the essential justification of a device such as the weekly broadsheet.

To substantiate this further, neo-literates clearly articulate the need for information to augment their income and to help them better cope with an control their immediate environment. The areas on which information is required are employment, market prices, medical and veterinary facilities, law & order situation, developmental schemes, loan schemes, government programmes and subsidies etc.

The publishing infrastructure in place

The current scenario regarding the availability of state or local newspaper in the districts is as follows:

No. of newspapers available

	Chit	Kam	Pan	Brdh	Durg
State level	8	5	5-7	4	1
Locally published	6	1	4	18	8

While there is some local facility in each district, the numbers very sharply, from a low of 1 to a high of 18.

In terms of production and distribution capabilities of the local infrastructure, an indicator is the circulation. The local circulation levels are as low as 1000 or less to a higher level of nearly 30,000 in a few cases. The norm is of the order of a few thousand only.

Most of the local district/block level newspapers operate at low profits and with a very limted infrastructure. The competition among them is very high.

Prima facie, there is capacity to print the broadsheet locally in all the districts except Panipat. Chittoor and Durg have modern offset printing facilities, while in Kamarajar, Bardhaman and Panipat, only the outdated letter press is available.

VIABILITY OF PUBLISHING & DISTRIBUTION

The response of the local newspapers to the idea of a weekly broadsheet for neo-literates is very positive, but only at a conceptual plane. There is a mixed response to the concrete scheme of publishing and distributing up to the village level.

The newspapers received the idea of publishing and distributing the broadsheet with a fair degree of enthusiasm. The motivation is both on the social and commerical fronts. The underlying social prestige and honour can be sensed, as well as the direct long term commercial gains. In their own words:

"It is a social reponsibility... and then the sale will also increase"

"As a social obligation I will do it"

"We will be indirectly canvassing our own newspaper"

"The reader base will increase"

However, they expressed their inability to reach the interior villages. Most of the newspapers in the districts have relatively low circulations. Their reach is restricted to block/ tehsil level or the villages situated on the periphery of the district headquarters/towns.

They expressed doubts about the commercial viability of broadening their existing distribution system to reach the far flung interior villages regularly. More so because of heavy competition at the district level, and the fear that it might result in delays in reaching their principal newspaper in time to their readers. This is compounded by the tight financial situation under which they operate.

These officials suggested that the broadsheet can be distributed through the existing network of NGO's associated with TLC, or through the infrastructure of the district administration. The broadsheet can also be posted directly to the neo-literates from the district level. Prima facie, the postal option seems fairly feasible since a ready mailing list at the village/ literacy centre level is easy to compile.

The cost of paper and printing the broadsheet ranges between Rs 225 and 500 per thousand copies (back to back) i.e. 25 to 50 paise per copy. The cost of distribution will be in addition.

Distributors of consumer products companies are negatively inclined to take up the distribution of a weekly broadsheet in view of infrastructural, reach and commercial constraints. Distributors who are presently distributing condoms etc as part of the social marketing programme of these companies, were of the view that the channel down the line take it as an "added burden". Therefore the trade network is unlikely to take up yet another 'product'.

Considering all these factors it seems at this juncture that the newspaper model is the most appropriate one. However, distribution up to the village level by a newspaper group is quite infeasible. To circumvent this problem, the postal option can be adopted. Then the broadsheet can be published even centrally by a mainline daily, at say the State capital.

Such a publisher will have the necessary wherewithal for large print runs and editorial infrastructure.

On the distribution aspect, we have discussed how to reach the braodsheet up to the village. The remaining issue is that of ensuring that from the village level it actually reaches the neo-literates. This is being addressed by NIAE separately.

CONTENTS OF THE BROADSHEET

To help in the choice of subjects and topics for the proposed broadsheet, experts, press and the neo-literates themselves were asked to give their opinions about the type of information and contemts relevant in this context. The following emerge as the more important areas for consideration:

- Information on agriculture e.g. advances made in implements, seeds, fertilizers etc.
- Local news from the state, block, district level and news on local/state level politics
- Information on various developmental schemes for women and weaker sections
- Employment news and prices of various commodities
- Educative real life stories, folk lore, mythology, stories about their kind of people
- Health related: treatment of various diseases, child health care, veterinary care
- Picture stories, stories for children
- Entertainment and sports, cinema news etc.
- News items on violence, murders, natural calamities, accidents, disasters etc

PROMISE OF THE CONCEPT

The overall response to the weekly broadsheet has been promising. The experts, newspapers and the neo-literates themselves are optimistic that it will definitely help the neo-literates to practice their acquired skills. Moreover they will have access to information on the various happenings outside their village. It will act as a window to the outside world. This can be a means of attaining the end objective of being empowered and attaining self reliance.

The beneficiaries have this to say:

"Good idea...lot of information"

"Will come to know of local news, nearby villages, blocks.... even at district/state level"

"Open our eyes to the outside world...expose us to new ideas"

"Will add to whatever we have learnt at the centre"

On the cirtical issue of pricing the broadsheet, we feel that a sensitive handling is imperative. The responses are mixed:

"Should be priced nominally" Panipat

"If distributed, people will certainly buy" Panipat

"Whatever I earn is not sufficient to feed myself, how can I pay for this" Kamarajar

"Connot pay...people cannot afford such things" Bardhaman

"Will certainly pay...worth it" Durg

It appears that price could pose to be a barrier in some areas, for example in the East and South, perhaps less so in the North. At this stage it might be a little risky to start with a priced publication. At a later stage, when the broadsheet enjoys a modicum of bebeficiary pull, the price issue can be considered. International experience indicates that this can work.

DIRECTIONS FROM THE STUDY-IN CONCLUSION

That the idea of the broadsheet stands ratified, can be stated with confidence. It is an appropriate route to encourage the practice of the newly acquired skills among neo-literates and help them to achieve the final goal of self reliance and a better economic status.

The newspaper model seems optimal, subject to certain conditions. Centralised publishing is seriously worth considering since the delivery mechanism is optimal via the postal route. This will take care of the editorial infrastructure and other facilities which most local groups are unlikely to have, and the comfort of financial backing and stability.

This however does not preclude the possibility of identifying competent local newspapers in some districts. The data base for this is available for the five TLC districts studied.

The research has provided broad cues to designing the content of the broadsheet in terms of the nature of the information and features. This should serve as the basis for further development, with additional inputs from formative research.

Initially it will be prudent not to price the broadsheet. Price could be considered at a later stage if the project meets with some success.

The last issue relates to reaching the broadsheet from the village or centre level to the neo-literates. A separate operations research has been conducted to provide inputs to resolve this issue.

19

FEED-BACK STUDY ON DAILY NEWSPAPERS/ BROADSHEET FOR NEO-LITERATES IN CHITTOOR AND NEELORE DISTRICTS OF ANDHRA PRADESH

Dr. C.K. Mohan Rao
Dr. M.V. Lakshmi Reddy

Experience shows shows that the neo-literates would relapse into illiteracy if they are not provided with interesting and relevant reading material. Retention and continuation of literacy skills acquired by the neo-literates during the literacy campaign and application of these skills for improving the personal and social life of neo-literates is a challenging task. To achieve this different learning strategies have been adopted by different TLC districts in post-literacy programmes. Supply of newspaper with reading mateiral specially designed for neo-literates is one such learning strategy.

Nellore and Chittoor districts in Andhra Pradesh are supplying reading materials to the neo-literates as a part of post-literacy programme. In both of these districts Telugu dailes carrying a special section for neo-literates and monitors are being supplied through the existing channel of newspaper net-work. In addition, a weekly boradsheet is also being supplied to the neo-literates in Chittoor district. In Nellore district, the special section for neo-literates is included in *Eenadu* and *Udayam* while the same is done by *Andhra Prabha* in Chittoor district. The content of the special section to the neo-literates, provided to the newspapers in Nellore district is prepared by

Zilla Saksharata Samithi (ZSS) whereas in Chittoor, the literacy news, covering wide range of issues and activites, published in *Andhra Prabha* daily, is defined by newspaper itself. The Chittoor ZSS has also developed a Weekly Broadsheet (WB) which is being supplied to the Jana Chaitanya Kendrams (JCKs) for use by neo-literates.

A study has been conducted in Nellore and Chittoor districts of Andhra Pradesh with a view to understand (1) distribution of these newspapers and broadsheet to JCKs and their accessibility to neo-literates, (2) the opinions of the neo-literates and monitors on language, content and presentation and (3) the suggestions offered by neo-literates for improvement. Initially, the intention was to examine the aspectes mentioned above, both in respect of the special section of the newspapers as well as the weekly broadsheet of Chittoor district. But at the time of study, in the month of July 1992, only three issues of broadsheet have come out and distribution was not yet been channelised. Therefore, the focus of the study was limited to the special section of newspapers meant for neo-literates. The study covered 40 neo-literates and 8 monitors in each district. Some of the important issues studied are as follows.

(A) DISTRIBUTION OF NEWS PAPERS

Regular and timely delivery of newspapers to the villages is a major concern as the existing newspapers have no network of agents in all the village of the districts. The study reveals that the newspapers are reaching most of villages on the same day and this is achieved through coordinated efforts of the existing newspaper network and the coordinators of ZSS at different levels. However, there are some problems in the distribution in 56% of the villages where newspaper has no agents of its own.

Circulation of newspapers/broadsheet among the neo-literates and villagers is another important issue which was studied. According to monitors the newspaper is generally delivered at JCK or at monitors house and on an average fifteen neo-literates attend JCK every day, half of them being women.

At the same time, some of the monitors complained that villagers are taking the newspaper to their houses or keeping it in places like tea shop, *grama chavidi*, etc. Monitors are not in a position to stop this practice and some times they are finding it difficult to get the paper by evening. It is also observed that the paper is accessibility is confined to only to males, if the monitor is male.

Monitors and neo-literates suggested that the newspaper should be sent through bus driver/conductor or postman for regular and timely supply to the villages where there are no agents. Similarly, they felt that the circulation of newspaper among neo-literates can be ensured by sending more number of copies to the village.

(B) RESPONSES OF NEO-LITERATES AND MONITORS

The responses of the neo-literates and monitors were elicited on daily newspapers. It was found that about 50% of neo-literates are not in a position to read independently the special section of the newspaper. They were getting assistance from others in reading and comprehending the material. Even those who are able to read the paper on their own had also some difficulty in understanding the content. In general, the majority of the neo-literates are reading the headings and the cinema titles in newspaper before going for the special section meant for them. Most of them could also tell the name of the special section.

The content of the special section of the newspapers in Nellore district covers one or two items every day like stories, folk songs, puzzles, jokes, health and sanitation, nutrition, agriculture, social evils, environment, politics, etc. Likewise one or two of the above items are covered under discussion forums and village parliaments in the special section of *Andhra Prabha* in Chittoor districts. Those neo-literates who are reading both the sections in Tirupathi edition felt that the *Akashara Deepam* is better than *Akshara Tapasman* with regard to the size of the letters as well as the content. In general, the stories are liked by the majority of the neo-literates. Most of the women showed greater liking for health and sanitation, and nutrition items while the men liked the items on agriculture and politics.

More than 52% of the neo-literates expressed that the language used in special section of the newspaper meant for neo-literates should be more simple. Only 10% of neo-literates suggested that is should be continued as it is. Only a few neo-literates felt the that language can be a little bit of higher standard. Where as nearly 60% of monitors felt that should be continued in the same standard as at present.

The majority of the neo-literates expressed satisfaction over content of the items in the special section and considered it as relevant and useful to their lives. Some suggested that the special section should also cover other items like child care, rural development, vocational training, etc.

They also suggested the special section to be made half page in the newspaper instead of quarter page as at present. In case of *Akshara Tapasman* majority of neo-literates and monitors suggested that it should be bold letter. In both the districts some neo-literates suggested the inclusion of pictures and cartoons.

WEEKLY BROADSHEET

With a view to provide useful and interesting reading material to neo-literates, ZSS, Chittoor has developed a Weekly Broadsheet for neo-literates on the lines of Weekly Broadsheet designed in Bengali by NIAE. Though it was intended to study Weekly Broadsheet in 'detail, it could not be done as only three issues were brought out by the time the study was launched. Moreover, the distribution was badly affected by transporters strike and reached only few JCKs. However, a sample of boradsheet carried by the investigator was given to neo-literates for reading and some information was collected thereafter.

The major problem in case of Weekly Broadsheet is its distribution because there is no network like agents of its own. In the begginning it was distributed through Mandal Development Officers which led to undue delay. So, recently ZSS has started sending the Broadsheet by post after having got concession on postage from postal department.

Regarding language, 9 out 14 neo-literates who read it, told that language used is simple and easy to read and comprehend. The contents of Weekly Broadsheet were also liked by neo-literates. Every issue of Broadsheet contains district news, functional and developmental information, health and child care, puzzles, jokes, etc. Majority of neo-literates are showing interest on stories and district news. Both neo-literates and monitors felt that presentation of Broadsheet is better than special section of newspaper as it is printed in bigger size letters with pictures and cartoons. As a whole, the Weekly Broadsheet is generally appreciated by all the neo-literates and monitors who read it.

20

NEWSPAPER FOR THE NEO-LITERATES

A Background Note on the NIAE Project on the Weekly Broadsheet (WB)

It is recognised that over the last few years, owning to the intensive efforts of the National Literacy Mission (NLM) and the total literacy compaign (TLC) in several districts a very large number of people have become literate. It is estimated that the total number of such neo-literate persons would be over 20 million. While they may be able to read and write it is possible that many of them are not self-reliant and therefore require to practice their acquired skills regularly. In the normal rural environment there is also not sufficient demand on the neo-literate persons to apply their skills. It is in this context that the need to read reading material to the neo literate persons become important. At the National Institute of Adult Education (NIAE) a specific experimental project was taken up to fill this void.

The objective of the project was to design and create enjoyable and appropriate reading materials for the neo-literate and ensure regular distribution and supply of such materials to the neo-literates persons on a continuing basis.

Further, the specific tasks to be accomplished were as follows:

i) To prepare 3-4 issues of a Weekly Broadsheet (WB) in Bengali, Telugu, Tamil and Hindi for the neo-literate based on field study and formative research among the intended readership in each language.

ii) To identify normal distribution channels for reaching the WB for the experimental project and demonstrate the viability for continued operation.

iii) To conduct and evaluation study among neo-literate persons to assess the effectiveness of the WB.

The first task was to design and prepare a Weekly Broadsheet (WB) in at least one language. Since, in Chittoor and Nellore Districts of Andhra Pradesh, some post-literacy programme was going on with one daily newspaper reaching every Jana Chaitanya Kendra (JCK) every day, it was felt that the exercise should be taken up in Bengali first, followed by Tamil and then Hindi and possibly Urdu. For this purpose, a brief formative research study was conducted in the Medinipur district of West Bengal to ascertain the literacy level of the neo-literate, their reading ability and preference of content. This was useful in guiding the preparation of the trial issue where the word-length of each item was kept to below 100 words and an attempt made to use very smple words and provide appropriate and locally specific information. The entire design of the Weekly Broadsheet (WB) has been an enage exercise in trying to give it the look of a complete newspaper and yet retaining some visual appeal and relevance for the neo-literate persons. The Tamil Weekly Broadsheet (WB) Thenril was similarly prepared based on some field visits, to a few districts in Tamil Nadu. However, no specific formative research was conducted to inquire into the preferences of the intended neo-literate readership. Both the Bengali and Tamil prototype Weekly Broadsheets-*JOG A JOG* and *THENRIL*-have been evaluated in few specific TLC districts where the post-literacy phase is operational.

The Hindi Weekly Broadsheet (WB) *Chahal-Pahal* has been prepared based on very detailed interaction with neo-literate women in Panipat (Haryana), Durg (Madhya Pradesh) and Banda (Uttar Pradesh). The main consideration is the design and selection of materials for the WB have been the subject preference of the neo-literate persons, particularly women who are a majority, viausl appeal and ease in reading and comprehension. The vocabulary, typography, format and layout have been guided by the expressed preferences of the neo-literate persons. Survey of other available materials for neo-literates and study of exiting newspaper style in the different language. Local specifications have been borne in mind, weightage given to appropriate information and enjoyable materials. While the effort has been to get away from dull development information it is interesting to note that the neo-literate persons themselves expressed their preferred need in terms of interesting, relevant day to day informatoon about the real world (agriculture, wages and prices, political news, home-based health care etc.)

The second task in connection with the Weekly Broadsheet (WB) was a study of the newspaper outreach/distribution system at below district level and exploring the willingness and capacity of the local newspapers to undertake the publication of the Weekly Broadsheet (WB). This research is being conducted by Mode Research in five districts -Panipat (Haryana), Durg (Madhya Pradesh), Burdwan (West Bengal), Chittoor (Andhra Pradesh) and Kamarajar (Tamil Nadu). The preliminary findings of the study indicates that the response to the idea of the Weekly Broadsheet (WB) is positive. However, the following issues have emerged for further consideration:

i) There does not appear to be any distribution system for reaching newspapers to the village level. News agents and hawkers are limited to towns and surrounding areas.

ii) The local newspapers operate on very small margins of profitability and are therefore reluctant to take on additonal responsibility of distribution. They would rather that it was done by the district authorities or through the postal system.

iii) However if the production and distribution costs are met, they are willing to take up the publication of the Weekly, Broadsheet (WB). As a matter of interest, the cost of production (paper and printing only) of 1000 copies of one sheet varies from Rs. 225 to Rs. 500. In some of the districts offset printing facility is available, while in others, only letter press is available.

iv) Capacity constraints exist and whether the district level newspapers will be able to gather the resources, including availability of newsprint, to bring out a Weekly Broadsheet (WB) of good quality on a regular basis remains a question mark.

In Chittoor and Nellore districts of Andhra Pradesh, the Zila Saksharta Samiti have identified a state-level newspaper that is being distributed to each of the post-literacy centres or Jana Chaitanya Kendras (JCKs) that have been set up in the two district. The identification of the particular newspaper (*Andhra Prabha* in Chittoor and *Eenaadu* in Nellore) was done on the basis of an open tender and open neogtiations with the news papers. The terms set down by the Zila Saksharta Samiti were the following :

i) The Tirupati edition of the daily newspaper must be reached to each of the JCK by the same evening. Payments will be made on certification of daily receipt from the JCK.

ii) One quarter page will be reserved for materials for neo-literates. in the case of Chittoor, the newspaper group produces the material which is essentially news and information from the JCKs. In the case of Nellore, the newspaper had deputed two persons from their staff to work with the ZSS to prepare a series of appropriate and graded learning materials for a period of time.

iii) There must be a price concession which worked out to approximately Rs. 1.25 per copy with about 8000-10000 JCK in each districts.

As a consequence of the NIAE effort to develop a prototype of a Weekly Broadsheet (WB) a Telugu prototype was developed locally in Chittoor under the guidance of the Zila Saksharta Samiti. *Velugu Bata* as the Weekly Broadsheet is called, was subsequently registered, as a newspaper and it is now being regularly distributed to all the post-literacy centres of the district. Each centre receives five copies of *Velugu Bata*. This clearly demostrated the technical feasibility of the WB effort at a district level. The National Literacy Mission is supporting the effort under the post-literacy programme of the district.

It must be clearly understood that the effort to produce and distribute a newspaper, with appropriate design/text for neo-literate persons, is independent of the specific post-literacy campaigns/programmes that are being designed in the TLC districts. It is an effort to open up a new viable mass media channel neglected. Special effort has to be made both in designing the appropriate format, text, layout and illustration and also in ensuring that the distribution channels are opened up such that the materials reach the village and then is further disseminated among the neo-literates. The effort at NIAE so far has been to tackle the design/editorial material and before long some design parameters would be found based on pretesting of the materials being prepared at NIAE. The Mode Research Study cited earlier has identified the problem of existing outreach of the newspaper distribution channels. Some further research will have to be done to understand the present machanism through which the newspaper that reaches the villages is then distributed among the neo-literates.

The problem at hand is to find the appropriate strategy so that a new media channel gets established independent of the post-literacy programme of NLM and thereby remains autonomous and so may continue even after the post-literacy programme is phased out in a district. The possible routes to establish this media channel are the following:

i) Some existing newspaper groups are encouraged to come forward to produce and distribute the newspaper. It would have to be persuasively argued that such a venture would be commercialy viable over a period of time.
ii) Facilitate the establishment of district/state level organisations (voluntary agencies or cooperatives) who would produce such a newspaper locally and over a period of time become self-reliant through advertisements and subscriptions.

specific needs and demands of the neo-literate audience have only recently begun to receive attention in this country. In order to further this work, NIAE has developed the Weekly Broadsheet Project as an experimental exercise in research, design and production of a newspaper that is appealing and useful for neo-literates. The emphasis has been on creating imaginative, injoyable, and locally relevant material and prototypes have been evolved in Bengali, Tamil and Hindi.

The experience has alrady been rewarding in many respects. It has strenghtened the awareness that there is a demand for creative reading material, not only form neo-literates but from the rural population in general. The design and editorial work has been particularly engrossing. Identifying, collecting and trying to present material in an interesting manner, at appropriate literacy levels was very challenging.

The content of the prototypes reflects a wide variety of issued--including political and development news, literacy news, stories, health and agricultural information, riddles and puzzles and other intractive exercise. In terms of design the effort has been to maintain the look of the newspaper.

OTHER EFFORTS

The response to NIAE's prototype broadsheet has been more than encouraging and many districts feel ready to take on the task of producing a similar paper (possibly with modifications) at the local/district level. Some have already begun. For instance in Chittoor at a similar Broadsheet being published and distributed regularly. In Tamil Nadu an independent group located in Pondicherry is trying to get together to carry forward the earlier initiative of developing a Tamil prototype. Aside from the broadsheet, a number of related initiatives are being planned in other parts of the country. For example in both Chittoor and Nellore districts of Andhra Pradesh a quarter page is set aside for neo-literates in maint stream daily news paper like *Andhra Prabha and Eenaadu.*

CROSSING THE HURDLES

There are many problem areas that need to be worked out. Broadly speaking, these are: problems related to distributions: getting together finances and costing (whether one approaches mainstream newspapers, advertisers, goverment funds); building an efficient publishing infrastructure, and developing an editorial infrastruscutre. While all these areas require urgent attention, problems related to the development of a strong editiorial and material support base are particularly pressing.

EDITORIAL CONCERNS

An area of concern that has been expressed by a number of people involved in the production of reading matter for neo-literates, is the difficulty they face in actually putting together material at the local level. Obviously the task becomes all the more difficult if such material is to be produced regualrly, for a weekly or daily broadsheet.

The problems are essentially two fold; a lack of resources and manpower, and a lack of access to wide variety of material, information bases and other related support services.

While at the district level compiling local news and other such relevant information and material is not a problem, procuring other features, news items, games or articles of interest may well be a problem. Our own experience of producing the various prototypes certainly confirms that the task of collecing interesting material is a time consuming and challenging one.

BRIDGING THE GAP: A FEATURES SERVICE

Although we have emphasized the distinctive problems of the broadsheet project as compared with conventional newspapers, problems of gathering sufficient reading matter on a regular basis are more or less universal. Perhaps surprisingly, even mainstream commercial dailies with their ample resources and large networks of correspondents and journalists are often hard pressed to provide enough material to fill their daily pages on a continous basis. What, they often rely on the bridge the gap, are the services of features services.

WHAT IS A FEATURES SERVICE

A features service provides newspapers and periodicals with a regular supply on material on an ongoing basis. Subscribers recieve regular access to a variety of information, features news brief etc. This saves them considerable expenditure on developing a large editiorial infrastructure.

For instance, most big newspapers (English) subscribe to the services of UNI and PTI to provide them with political news items and other government information. Besides this there are a number of other professionally run services that provide very specialized services. For instance features on women, sports, development or environment. Therefore in its essentials a features service is a centrally run professional outfit with a wide network providing a specific and specialized service.

EXPLORING THE OPTION OF A NEWS FEATURES SERVICES FOR NEO LITERATES:

The question before us then is the relevance of such a concept for a product that is qualitatively different from a mainstream newspaper.

IS THERE A ROLE FOR CENTRALLY DISTRIBUTED MATERIAL?

It has often been asserted, and rightly so, that the acceptablity and success of a broadsheet for neoliterates depends on providing locally relevant material reflecting the local culture and written in the idiom of the region. While the importance of this can hardly be denied it is equally true that a broadsheet must have a wide variety of material that will appeal to a large cross section of people. Therefore, besides local information it must also contain items on health, environment, information related to agricultural developments, animal husbandary, general development information, women related stories, legal information, puzzles, games and other interesting features. Much of this kind of information is not region specific, but could be adapted to suit the needs of a particular area. The need for centrally disseminated material and therefore for an agency to provide this service cannot be dismissed.

The premise of such an effort would be based on building strong networking channels. Once established these will be condiuts for sharing news, grass roots experiences stories and folk tales (to mention a few possible tacks). This would naturally allow for access to a much larger resource pool and a richer fund of experiences. It could broaden the scope of the broadsheets from beyond the bounds of particular districts and provide neo-literates with a wider exposure.

PREVENTING DUPLICATION OF EFFORT-MAINTAINING QUALITY

One advantage of this approach is that it would minimize the duplication of effort. If in each district planning a broadsheet, people were to be engaged in indentifying and then writing this kind of material there would be a considerable amount of duplicated effort. Moreover availing of the expertise and information from a larger network would help maintain standards. Such a facility would provide local editorial groups with a much larger range of material to choose from, without any compromise being made in the final selection of items and the manner in which they will ultimately be made available.

LONG TERM PLANNING

One of the drawbacks of working for single issue (as we have learned from developing prototypes) is that there is little scope for long term-planning and in many cases the selection of items might be at random. On the other hand, the possibility of a regular features service allows for say, a well thought out series on health realted issues. Or, for instance, it might be possible to develop certain characters talking about various issues (corruption, gender discrimination etc) which could be used regularly in the broadsheets. once these are establishment, readers begin to look forward to reading what they have to say in very issue.

Moreover, the establishment of a such a centralized organization would allow for linkages with other professional bodies. To cite an example, an area of interest expressed during the formative research in Bengali, was information on weather. In such a case a regular arrangement could be made with the Meteoroligical Office which is a centrally located body and the information disseminated. A similar case could be made for the demand often made by neo-literates to publish prices of agricultural products and other essential commodities.

PROVIDING SUPPORT : A POSSIBLE ROLE FOR NIAE

NIAE is not in a position to engage in the actual production of the broadsheet. Having initiated a process however, it is important for NIAE to continue actively providing support to others taking up the venture. One area where we can provide active assitance is in getting together and disseminating materials to those engaged in producting such material. Being placed in Delhi, and with access to resources that district personnel might not have, NIAE can work towards putting together regular packages of material. In other words functioning as a specialized news features service of sorts.

SOME CONCRETE SUGGESTIONS

Collecting Material:-

WRITTEN MATERIAL-

They type of items that the news service could provide are special features, women's stories, environment news, information on new agricultural developments, health, legal information, interactive exercise, games and puzzles, stories riddles. Material elicited from other agencies like the Meteorological Office etc.

VISUAL MATERIAL:

Photographs as well as other illustrated material could be provided. Additionally developing a regular comic strip might be looked into.

LANGUAGE

We could provide a bilingual facility, providing the information in Hindi and English (for non-Hindi speaking areas). Tranlations into local dialect and final presentation could be done in a decentralized manner.

PRESENTATION

There are two aspects that have to be looked into;

Properly edited background material on various issues can be provided to the user to be modified and used by them.

Items written in a format suitable for neoliterates would also be provided. This would naturally be simply written, short items.

CIRCULATION

Likely subscribers to the service need to be identified before evolving a systematic dissemination system. This would involve networking with different invididuals, voluntary agencies, SRC's TLC districts etc. An exhaustive mailing list would have to be created. As mentioned earlier the importance and willingness of various partners to regularly send in material which could them be disseminated would be a key factor in ensuring the success of such an idea.

PERIODICITY

A monthly package could be sent out to the subscribers to be used by them whenever appropriate. As the items will mostly not be news items the problem appropriate timings would not be a consideration.

In conclusion it must be reiterated that this is not a final blue print for a course of action. Rather it is the culmination of insights gathered while working on this project and interacting with a large number of people involved in similar ventures and must be seen in that context.